C000212369

'Duncan's words pulsate with l
again that to be truly alive is to let
of our existence. Here are the wor
God's presence to become his pr
shape his daily choices. Wholehea..... .... me into greater
intimacy with God, greater freedom in God and greater hope
from God. Chapter by chapter, line by line, sometimes word by
word, Duncan weaves a tapestry of possibility. His book lifts
our vision of what it means to flourish toward heaven while
rooting us in the here and now of God's kingdom. If we will let
it, *Wholehearted* will liberate us from the mediocrity of
programmed, predictable Christianity and propel us into the
wild, beautiful landscape of a soul captivated by God. Not what
God can do, not what God commands, not even what God
requires, but God: the Father who loves us, the Son who
embraces us, and the Spirit who transforms us. He calls us to be
people whose hearts are set on God, and Christ-followers who
love God above everything else. It's a beautiful, evocative and
live-giving book, a breathing hole for those whose relationships
with God have become frozen by predictability.'
Malcolm Duncan, pastor, author and international speaker

'When someone we respect asks us to prioritise something
"above all else", it leaves little room for any ambiguity of its
importance. The book of Proverbs says, 'Above all else, guard
your heart' (Proverbs 4:23) – but just how do we do this?
Wholehearted answers this question, and it does so with beautiful
clarity, accessibility and insight. This great resource illuminates
the inner part of our lives, giving us an opportunity to be
searched and empowered for greater fruitfulness. This book will
both search and inspire you to be "wholehearted".

   'The best books I have read don't just address interesting
topics or contain well-written thoughts, but they also flow
authentically from the writer's heart and experience. This book
has been lived by Duncan and has overflowed to the pages of

this book. I believe it will also overflow to the reader and help them live "wholehearted" lives for God.'
Mark Pugh, Lead Pastor, Rediscover Church, Exeter

'*Wholehearted* has been both an inspiring and challenging read. Duncan has captured so beautifully what it means to be completely sold out to the Lord in this day and age. My heart has been so stirred by this book. I believe it will be a blessing to anyone seeking to go deeper in their relationship with the Lord.'
James Aladiran, Founder and Director of Prayer Storm

'Amen! This is the word that best captures my reaction to the insights mirrored in the pages of this book, which I found to be such a sincere invitation for inward looking at life. My dear friend Duncan discusses germane points and provides pertinent life principles based on reflection on Caleb's life and his ministry experiences as well as an earnest desire to live a life of wholeheartedness – a life worthy to live.

'Indubitably, this work is a great reminder that life is a function of heart. Life is shaped, lived and destined by the condition of heart. What is saved in the heart either saves or destroys life, depending on its source. When the heart is properly guarded, life is guarded. These and so many more nuggets of truth/wisdom are judiciously explained and readily available, to be mined during a time intentionally allotted for self-reflection in the presence of God's word and the Holy Spirit. This is not only a book, but also an honest friend, that speaks the truth in love. My earnest appreciation to Duncan for this work and for the invaluable friendship in the Lord and in ministry particularly to children.'
Tsehaywota Taddesse, National Director, Compassion International Ethiopia Office

'This timely and engaging book has designs on us. It is literally after our hearts. Duncan asks practical but penetrating questions not just about what has been but about what life could be like from now on. What if every follower of Jesus chose to live a life of full devotion? What if every local church was serious about living wholeheartedly for Jesus and serving Him unreservedly in their community? Duncan invites us to believe that the God who stirs and speaks to our heart will also renew our hearts and enable us to live wholeheartedly for Him for the rest of our lives. Read it and tell all your friends.'

Chris Cartwright, General Superintendent, Elim

'Duncan has written a book that will inspire and equip you to wholehearted living. From years of personally putting this into practice, he offers us insight, wisdom and practices that we can embed into our own discipleship and leadership. Many of us begin with wholehearted devotion, and this book, drawing on the life of Caleb, is an opportunity to review and reset. As you prayerfully read this book, may you be drawn into an ever-deepening relationship with the One who calls us to follow and walks with us on the journey.'

Sarah Whittleston, Co-Lead Pastor, Elim Life Church; National Prayer Leader, Elim Prayer

WHOLEHEARTED

Giving our everything to the One
who is our everything

Duncan Clark

instant
apostle

First published in Great Britain in 2021

Instant Apostle
104 The Drive
Rickmansworth
Herts
WD3 4DU

Every effort has been made to seek permission to use copyright material reproduced in this book. The publisher apologises for those cases where permission might not have been sought and, if notified, will formally seek permission at the earliest opportunity.

The views and opinions expressed in this work are those of the author and do not necessarily reflect the views and opinions of the publisher.

British Library Cataloguing-in-Publication Data

A catalogue record for this book is available from the British Library.

This book and all other Instant Apostle books are available from Instant Apostle:

Website: www.instantapostle.com

Email: info@instantapostle.com

ISBN 978-1-912726-46-2

Printed in Great Britain.

To: Family
You have created a loving foundation from which I can flourish.

To: Friends
You have cheered me on to become the best version of me I can be.

To: Coventry Elim
You have taught me how to live and lead wholeheartedly.

For the eyes of the LORD range throughout the earth to strengthen
those whose hearts are fully committed to him.
2 Chronicles 16:9

Contents

Foreword

This book is a timely, biblical, clear and costly call about what it truly means to follow Jesus. My friend Duncan provides such an important challenge to us all in a way that is accessible, practical and grounded. The overarching invitation of the book to 'give the whole of your life to a cause that is greater than yourself' explodes from every page. It's not a new challenge, but is written in a way that has fresh impetus for today. The call is clear for us to stand out and be distinct in our time. After all, the Church was never intended to fit in with no differentiation between her and the society she inhabits. We are not called to become magnolia wallpaper on the world's agenda but instead to be a part of the world, but distinct within it. Duncan makes this very clear and shows us afresh that Christians should be influencers in our world, not the influenced. We want to be bringing others along with us as opposed to being drawn along with them. We should be following the way of Christ, which will often be directly counter to the cultural norm. This book highlights the excitement of living this kind of life, and not just the cost.

We are here to flavour the world and bring about difference within it. We must be salt that hasn't lost its flavour and light that hasn't run out of battery! We can be confident too that however hard it is to be distinct, Jesus is with us. In those places where it feels impossible, there He is. In those times we feel most marginalised, He stands with us. In those moments of our greatest victories, there too is He.

This call to live a life sold out to Jesus is so timely in our culture. As I read this book, I found my love for Jesus growing. The challenge to be more on fire for the Lord was clear. It reminded me of a time when I had an amazing meeting with a passion expert. I'm already fairly naturally passionate, but nonetheless I was keen to hear from her about what makes people passionate and how you can tell what their passions are. She asked me, simply, if I knew how one could tell what people are passionate about. I gave myself a moment to think, then answered, 'I reckon that what they spend their money on is a fairly good clue.' She shut me down and said that my answer could literally not be more wrong. What we spend our money on is entirely socially conditioned, apparently!

I did want the actual answer, though, so I said, 'OK, then, how do you tell?' She said to me there are two simple ways.

1. What people spend their time on. Time is so precious and you only give significant amounts of it to the things you really have to.
2. What people talk about. Apparently, it's impossible to have a half-hour conversation with someone and not hear out of their mouth what they are primarily passionate about.

I came away from this encounter deeply challenged. Am I that passionate about Jesus? Does my time reflect this passion? Can someone spend thirty minutes with me in conversation and fail to hear about Jesus? Over the time that's followed I've often tested in conversation the thirty-minute rule. It has never failed to prove correct that in having a chat of this length with someone, you always hear their primary passions through the natural course of the conversation.

This book had a similar challenge for me. Am I on fire enough, committed enough, distinct enough, passionate enough for the world around me to notice and be impacted? I long to be part of a Church today in the UK that, like the early Church, has that unstoppable urge to tell other people about the Jesus they've met who has changed everything about them.

We are living in challenging times. The recovery from a global pandemic as well as a secular tsunami within our culture are just some of what lies in front of the UK Church. However challenging the landscape looks, though, I remain wholeheartedly convinced that it's through the Church that this nation will be transformed. After all, it's only Christ who can provide hope to the hopeless, a family to the lonely and isolated, and restoration to the broken. We, the Church, are His bride, called to be His hands and feet, and His ambassadors, activists and workers in our communities. This book has the potential to awaken many more of us to live the kind of lives that can lead to us being the Church needed in this cultural moment. It may take many years but we must be a Church living wholeheartedly for Christ for the long term.

I'm grateful to Duncan for the focus he places on our hearts in this book. He makes the importance of this clear and gives practical help for us to transform our hearts into greater Christ-likeness. Rich in Scripture, practical and challenging, I believe this book will have a profound impact on your life. As I finished it, I felt a fresh stirring to be a Caleb in my generation. My prayer is that when you finish it, you will feel the same.

Gavin Calver
CEO, Evangelical Alliance

Prelude I

Caleb

I, however, followed the LORD my God wholeheartedly.[1]

Not all people are born equal.

At least, that's how it appears.

Some are born for the spotlight; others are more comfortable in the shadows. Even some of the Bible's most well-known characters seemed to be content to live their lives in the shadow of those whose achievements appeared greater than their own. Their names are on the Bible's B-list rather than the A-list. Jonathan's story of loyalty is overshadowed by David's giant-killing. Joseph's story of integrity is eclipsed by Mary's selection to give birth to the Messiah.

Caleb joins Jonathan and Joseph on the Bible's B-list.

Caleb lived his life in the shadow of Joshua, Israel's impressive warrior-leader. Joshua learned leadership as Moses' personal assistant. Joshua fought great battles,

---

[1] Joshua 14:8.

captured cities, devised strategy, conquered land. Joshua finds himself on the A-list.

Caleb found himself in Joshua's shadow, but it didn't bother him one bit. His goal was never power, popularity or fame. He set his sights on something greater than those temporary earth-bound achievements. Caleb aimed for full devotion. Total commitment to the pursuit of God and His purposes.

Caleb emerges from the shadows, stands out from all his peers and boldly declares, 'I'm going after wholehearted living.' He resists any drift towards a lukewarm life. He rejects the allure of comfort. Caleb determines to give every part of himself to one goal: the wholehearted quest of knowing God deeply and serving Him fully.

At the age of eighty-five, at a time in life when some of us could be looking back on a decade or two of golfing and garden centres, Caleb is still full of the fight. He's still got courage to take on the giants. He's still got passion for the cause.

For forty-five of those years he's been surrounded by a community full of people who doubt, criticise and complain; but Caleb maintains his full devotion to God. For four decades he has dug thousands of graves for his friends and family as they have died in the desert; but Caleb continues to passionately pursue God's purposes. Even when the battles are intense, the losses are great and resources are running low, Caleb stands to his feet and declares, 'I … followed the LORD my God wholeheartedly.'

This book is an invitation to live like Caleb.

It is an invitation to give the whole of your life to a cause that is greater than yourself.

It is an invitation to see what others can't see; to live how others don't live; to stand out rather than blend in.

It is an invitation to live from the inside out, with a full and healthy heart.

It is an invitation to live with passion, to stay the course and to finish well.

It is an invitation to wholehearted living for the long term.

As you read this book, your goal is not to reach the back page in record time. The goal is the transformation of your heart. There comes a time in most of our lives when making small adjustments is not enough. We wake up one day and realise that we must rearrange our lives for the reordering of our hearts. The aim of this book is to provoke you to do just that.

So slow down.

Resist the temptation to rush.

Pause at the end of each chapter.

Take a few deep breaths.

Become aware of God's presence.

Ask Him what He wants to say to you.

Expect your heart to be changed.

Prelude II

Habits of the Heart

I am a middle-aged man.

I don't know how it happened, but one day I woke up to discover I was no longer twenty-one but in my mid-forties. Time flies.

There are a few benefits to reaching mid-life – only a few. One is, I am now entitled to a free over-forties' health check. Since it was free, I booked in.

I entered the doctor's office expecting a full and thorough physical examination. That didn't happen. Instead, the doctor asked me multiple questions about my lifestyle. She asked me whether I smoked, whether I drank alcohol, how much exercise I took, and whether I preferred pizza and kebabs to lettuce leaves and pumpkin seeds. Good questions.

The doctor was making an assessment of the condition of my heart based on my lifestyle habits. She knew that if I lived well, my heart would be well.

The same principle that we apply to the physical can be applied to the spiritual.

Many years ago, I learned that *I become what I repeat.* That the rhythms and routines that I choose, either intentionally or accidently, have a profound impact upon the kind of person I become and the condition of my heart; the core of who I am from which everything else in my life flows.

Throughout this book you will see an emphasis on the importance of your heart (more about the meaning of 'the heart' coming up shortly!) and a frequent call to wholehearted living which will require you to consider the health of your heart. I've grown to believe that *if you value your heart it will be visible in your habits.*

With that in mind, each chapter will conclude with suggested 'Habits for the heart' that, if repeated regularly, I believe will play an important part in you presenting yourself to God, opening your heart to His transforming power and increasing your awareness of His presence.

There are times when I believe that I can independently transform my own heart. That is a delusion. Transformation built on a New Year's resolution nearly always fails. Apart from the presence of Jesus, real and lasting change cannot happen. Heart habits open my inner world and invite Him to come near.

When consistently practised, these habits become ingrained in our bodies and minds. They form part of the everyday routine of our lives so that we no longer have to think too much about them. They become the normal way of our living and being in this world.

For some of you, these 'Habits for the heart' will provoke you to make some very minor adjustments to your daily or weekly schedule. For others, they will prompt you to radically reorder your life so that you can more intentionally listen to the longings of your heart and rearrange your life for spiritual seeking.

I'll leave that up to you!

1

Wholehearted

There is more than one way you can live your life.

You can choose the path of least resistance. You can choose to set comfort as your goal. You can live a risk-averse life of pain avoidance. You can choose half-hearted living. And if you choose to live that kind of life, I can hardly blame you. I mean, who really wants to live a life where you might experience failure, pain and insurmountable challenges?

The problem is, if you choose to live half-hearted, you can end up living a half-life.

There is another way to live. We'll call it 'wholehearted living'. It requires the passionate pursuit of one thing for the long term. And while it is a life of focus and desire, it would be a mistake to think it is a driven life or that it demands the lifestyle of a workaholic. It is not a life of ruthless striving or self-centred grasping. It is a life built on a foundation of trust and rest. On top of that foundation, the wholehearted person constructs a way of living where they give the *whole* of themselves to the pursuit of God and all that He has for the one and only life they have been given.

That's the kind of life that this book invites you to live.

I'm a preacher. I've been taught to always ask people to open – or turn on – their Bibles whenever I have the privilege to teach.

Please turn to Joshua 14. (Sorry, I can't help it!)

Here are Israel's oldest members. Joshua and Caleb have been through four and a half decades of pain. Forty years of aimlessly wandering around a soulless desert. Five years of fights and battles; losses and victories. At a time when you and I would probably be implementing our retirement plans, these two legends are discussing land and how they can conquer more of it. They are strategising for their next battle. They have no plans to retreat.

Caleb speaks up. He reflects on the struggles and successes of the last forty-five years and lets us know how he navigated the ups and downs of wars and wanderings: 'I, however, followed the LORD my God wholeheartedly.'[2]

Even though others doubted and wanted to return to Egypt, I still followed the Lord my God wholeheartedly.

Even though we lost some painful battles, I still followed the Lord my God wholeheartedly.

Even though I'm eighty-five years old, I still have the energy for the fight, still have the courage to take on the giants, still have

---

2 Joshua 14:8.

passion for the cause. I'm still following the Lord my God wholeheartedly.

I'm impressed! Aren't you?

But Caleb's wholehearted devotion to God doesn't just become evident when he puts eighty-five candles on his birthday cake. His wholehearted faith drew God's attention forty-five years earlier.

Please turn to Numbers 13 and 14. (Again, I apologise, but I can't help it!)

If you were ever sent to Sunday school as a child, you'll probably remember the story well. Moses has led the people of Israel to the edge of the Promised Land. He sends in twelve spies to check out the land in preparation for their military assault.

Ten were bad. Two were good.

Ten see the problems. Two focus on the promises.

Ten say, 'We can't do it.' Two say, 'We can do it.'

Ten say, 'They are giants and they will crush us like grasshoppers under their size-twenty feet.' Two say, 'With God on our side, it's a no-brainer.'

The two? Joshua and Caleb, of course.

In that moment, Caleb's self-declaration of wholehearted living is trumped by God's description of this faith-filled visionary:

> My servant Caleb has a different spirit and follows me wholeheartedly, I will bring him into

27

the land he went to, and his descendants will inherit it.[3]

Notice that word again? *Wholehearted.*

When everyone else doubted, when everyone else lacked faith for the fight, when everyone else wanted to throw in the towel and quit, Caleb stood out from his contemporaries because of his relentless, full devotion to God.

It may be a total coincidence, but some scholars point out that Caleb's name, in the original Hebrew language, means 'dog'. Strange, I know! (I mean, if you were to name your child after an animal, Tiger, Lion or Bear might be good choices. But Dog?) It may appear a strange choice to us, but maybe Caleb's parents were following the biblical pattern of giving their child a name that made a prophetic declaration over their future.

I know very little about dogs, but I do know that they tend to be admired for their loyalty and devotion to their master. That's why we have guide dogs and rescue dogs, and not rescue cats! In fact, someone has said that the one big difference between dogs and cats is that dogs will worship you while cats will expect you to worship them.

It may just be a coincidence, but Caleb lived up to the meaning of his name. It was like he was God's dog, loyally and wholeheartedly following his Master.

Wholehearted.

I think it's time for a definition.

In fact, that one word looks like it should be two words, which might help us.

---

[3] Numbers 14:24.

Whole.

Heart.

That word 'whole' reminds us of something the entirety of Scripture teaches us, that God demands the whole of us, not just part of us.

The writer of Proverbs instructs us to 'Trust in the LORD with *all* [our] heart'[4], as opposed to a part of our heart.

When Jesus was questioned about which of the commandments He perceived to be the most important, He responded by saying, 'Love the Lord your God with *all* your heart and with all your soul and with all your mind and with all your strength.'[5]

It's difficult to ignore the word 'all' in those ancient texts because they remind us that God requires us to give the whole of our lives as we follow Him. Body. Mind. Soul. Heart. The whole lot. All in.

I grew up with stories ringing in my ears of Christ-followers giving their whole lives as they followed hard after God. No half measures.

In my teens I was told the story of American missionary, Jim Elliot, who was speared to death in 1956 by Auca Indians as he followed God's call to tell this unreached people group about the love of Jesus. A few days before his death he wrote in his journal, 'He is no fool who gives what he cannot keep to gain what he cannot lose.'[6]

That's *wholehearted* language.

---

[4] Proverbs 3:5, italics mine.

[5] Mark 12:30, italics mine.

[6] E Elliot, *In the Shadow of the Almighty* (New York City: Harper & Row, 1958), p174.

Around the same time, I was handed a book about a very English gentleman called C T Studd who was born into a wealthy family, studied at the University of Cambridge and played cricket for England. Yet, in the early part of the twentieth century, Studd realised his faith demanded full devotion to God. He followed a missionary call to China and India, penning these words in his letters home, 'If Jesus Christ is God and died for me, then no sacrifice is too great for me to make for Him.'[7]

That's *wholehearted* language.

It's not that long ago that I read the inspiring biography of Dietrich Bonhoeffer, a German theologian and pastor who lived and ministered in Nazi Germany in the Second World War. His strong Christian faith and opposition of Hitler eventually led him to a concentration camp in Flossenburg where he was executed by hanging on 9th April 1945. Shortly before his death he wrote, 'When Christ calls a man, he bids him, "Come and die."'[8]

That's *wholehearted* language.

It may be ridiculously obvious, but I need to say it: wholehearted living requires the whole of you. It requires all of you. Which makes me wonder; when you read the word 'all', what is it about that word that makes you feel uncomfortable?

Do you feel uncomfortable because it includes your money?

Your time?

---

[7] N Grubb, *C. T. Studd: Cricketer and Pioneer* (Fort Washington, PA: Christian Literature Crusade, 1933), p124.

[8] D Bonhoeffer, *The Cost of Discipleship* (London: SCM Press, 2006), p44.

Your career?

Your family?

Your attitude?

All means *all*. *Whole* means *whole*. Everything. Nothing left out.

And then there's that second word:

Heart.

Of course, when the Bible uses the word '*heart*' it is rarely referring to the blood-pumping muscle that you hope is beating rhythmically somewhere inside your chest right now. It usually refers to the unseen core of who you are. It's that complex combination of your thoughts, emotions, desires, understanding and will. It's your inner world. Your centre.

To put it simply, you live from the heart.

Whatever's going on in your heart will spill out. Solomon called it 'the wellspring of life' (Proverbs 4:23, TPT) because he knew that every part of our life is affected by the overflow from our hearts. Unless our hearts are reformed by the intentional habits we adopt, unredeemed patterns of thinking and behaving will rise to the surface and will win the day.

Most people I know are incredibly polite. They are nice people.

Until something goes wrong.

Until their car breaks down. Until their children have a tantrum in the frozen-food aisle of the local supermarket. Until they are running late and have a difference of opinion with their spouse in the car on the way to church. In those moments, what is in their heart overflows.

You may be able to hide the things you have done, but you can never hide what is in your heart because it will always spill out in your words and your actions.

At school, I received a detention because I threw my friend's bag out of the classroom window, but I hid the detention slip from my parents and told them I was at cricket practice so that they would never know what I had done (until now). Not the greatest crime, I know, but you get the point.

You can hide the things you've done from the people in your life who matter most, but you can never cover up the condition of your heart because it will always overflow.

We live from our hearts.

We live from the inside out. Even though we spend large amounts of time improving our *outside*, it is our *inside* that drives us. Even though we live in a culture that gives priority to the mind, to intellectual pursuits and academia, it is from the heart that we make our choices, take steps into action and try to influence our bit of the world.

I don't need to tell you – but I will – that living with a healthy heart, overflowing with full devotion to God for the long term, isn't the easiest thing to maintain. Our hearts get easily damaged. Our hearts get broken. Our hearts grow cold. Our hearts get hardened. Our hearts become hurried and harassed.

Maybe that's why Caleb's example is so impressive?

Wholehearted devotion to God for the long term.

The whole of his life, lived from a healthy heart, decade after decade, without ever letting up.

And so, we arrive at a couple of important questions that underpin the entire content of this book:

What does it take to follow the Lord wholeheartedly for the long term?

What did it take for Caleb to maintain full devotion to God for more than four decades from Numbers 14 through to Joshua 14?

I love to run.

In fact, running has become almost an addiction for me (don't judge me; there are worse addictions I could have chosen, let me assure you).

For more than a decade now I have risen early to run. Eighty per cent of my days I have rolled out of bed before my family gets up and I've spent the first hour or so of my day with a mixture of Bible reading, prayer and running. I've found the running element of my early mornings to be a vital spiritual practice for me as I centre my soul in the relative stillness of my city at that time of day.

In this last decade or so I've run some marathons, half-marathons and this wonderful thing called ParkRun where more than 700 people meet each Saturday morning (apart from when a global pandemic stops us!) and we run or walk – or race – a five-kilometre route around my local park. I've run the same ParkRun route more than 250 times and I've noticed the same thing happen every week: there are people who sprint like crazy for the first mile but run out of energy for the second mile and I catch them up and overtake them on the second lap of the park. It happens every single week.

What is the point of starting well if you can't finish strongly?

Some of you who are reading this book are likely to be young adults and you have some great dreams and goals for your life. You have in your mind some of the great things you would like to achieve with your life. Some of you have already decided to fully devote yourself to knowing and following Jesus Christ.

I want you to know that I'm cheering you on!

But I also want you to know that you are entering into a way of life that doesn't just require you to start well; it also calls you to finish well, with the same level of passion that you started with (or even more!). Many people can sprint the first 100 metres of the marathon. Starting well is easy.

It is also possible that some of you who have picked up this book are, like me, closer to half-time. You are midway through the race and you find yourself carrying loads of things that have the potential to slow you down and deplete the energy you can give to full devotion to God.

Those things are often good things.

Maybe you got married. Maybe you remained single. Some of you will have built a successful career. Others will have had children. Some of you will have taken on a mortgage. Still others will have wrestled with unemployment. I appreciate that each person who reaches half-time carries their own unique weight of joys and challenges, but I find that at this stage of life some will start to feel that their limitations outnumber their options. The dreams they had in their twenties have started to fade and they're wondering if they have the energy to live a life that looks anything like wholehearted.

I get that.

Then, of course, there are some who are taking the time to read this book and you sense you are getting closer to the finish line. For some, the challenge with drawing nearer to the finish line is that you start to notice all those young people who are taking your place, and they are doing the things you used to do in ways that you would never have dreamed of doing them.

You may even start to ask yourself, 'Is anyone aware of what I once did or who I once was?' It's possible that you will limp towards the finish line wrestling with irritability, anger and sadness, rather than with that wholehearted devotion to Christ you once had.

Please don't finish the race like that.

For me, one of the most heart-breaking things I've witnessed in recent years has been leaders who fall at the last hurdle. They are only a few metres from the finish line and then something in their character or in their conduct disqualifies them from crossing the line with joy. It's so painful to see.

If you are a leader, please don't finish your race like that.

Whether you find yourself on the start line, at half-time or near the finish line, wholehearted living is within your reach. It has nothing to do with striving and everything to do with surrender as you invite God to do a bit of heart surgery.

As this chapter draws to an end, maybe those of you who find yourselves at the start of your race might declare this prayer to God:

I'm all in. I'm devoting the whole of my life to follow You.

Those of you who would find yourselves in the middle of the race, maybe open your heart and say to God:

I have no plan to quit at half-time. I have every desire, with Your help, to live wholeheartedly for the long term.

And for those of you who sense that you're closer to the finish line than you are to half-time, perhaps whisper this prayer to God:

I am going to finish well. I have every intention of finishing this race with even more faith, hope and love than I started with.

There is more than one way you can choose to live your life.

Wholehearted is one way.

You choose.

Habits for the heart

One of the most beneficial habits that a follower of Christ can add to their daily or weekly rhythm is what is often called 'journalling'.

It is very simple and uncomplicated.

Just find an empty diary or notebook and use it to record God's activity in your life. Every time you write an entry in your journal, open it to a blank page, write today's date and then scribble down whatever is on your heart.

You might want to write out an honest prayer. You might want to record something you sense God has been saying to you. You might write a list of the things that you are thankful for. You might write out a verse or two from the Bible that has been important to you lately.

If you're really struggling to know where to start, take the words of Psalm 139:23-24 and use them as a prayer:

> Search me, God, and know my heart;
> test me and know my anxious thoughts.
> See if there is any offensive way in me,
> and lead me in the way everlasting.

Then open your journal to a blank page and let the words flow.

2

A Battle-ready Heart

'You cut, I choose.'

Have you ever used that age-old statement for the fair and envy-free division of just about anything that can be cut in two?

Often, it's cake.

Two siblings spy the last piece of lonely chocolate gateau on the plate and the wise parent maintains family harmony by suggesting that one child takes the job of cutting, the other child choosing.

The fair division of cake is simple. The fair division of land, less so.

Let's jump back into Joshua 14. The two veterans of Israel, Joshua and Caleb, are having a conversation about the distribution of the land; about who gets what:

> Now the people of Judah approached Joshua at Gilgal, and Caleb son of Jephunneh the Kenizzite said to him, 'You know what the LORD said to Moses the man of God at Kadesh Barnea about you and me. I was forty years old when Moses the servant of the LORD sent me from Kadesh

Barnea to explore the land. And I brought him
back a report according to my convictions.'[9]

Once again, Caleb is taking us back to the 'ten were bad,
two were good' story of Numbers 13 and 14. You'll
remember that Caleb was one of the two good guys who
brought their undercover surveillance report back to
Moses. I love the way he delivered it, 'according to my
convictions'. This is the way another version puts it, 'I
brought back word to him *as it was in my heart.*'[10]

Caleb had seen that the land was full of giants and that
the enemy was too strong for them, but that didn't deter
him because in his heart he knew that God would fight for
them. Caleb had an inner conviction that the battle was the
Lord's and that there was no enemy – no matter how tall
or strong they might be – that the Lord couldn't overcome!

The text, and Caleb, continues, 'but my fellow Israelites
who went up with me made the hearts of the people
sink'.[11]

Notice the heart posture of the people.

They were convinced that the enemy was too strong,
that the giants were too big, that there was no way they
could win and that they would have been better off in
Egyptian slavery.

Their hearts sink.

They have no hope in their hearts. No belief that God is
big enough to rescue them or fight for them. Their heart
posture is one of defeat.

---

[9] Joshua 14:6-7.
[10] Joshua 14:7, NKJV, italics mine.
[11] Joshua 14:8.

Contrast that with the posture of Caleb's 'heart':

> I, however, followed the LORD my God
> wholeheartedly. So on that day Moses swore to
> me, 'The land on which your feet have walked
> will be your inheritance and that of your
> children for ever, because you have followed the
> LORD my God wholeheartedly.'[12]

Caleb's heart is full of faith and trust. Even though the enemy is strong, he wholeheartedly believes that God is stronger and that the victory will be His.

Caleb continues:

> Now then, just as the LORD promised, he has
> kept me alive for forty-five years since the time
> he said this to Moses, while Israel moved about
> in the wilderness. So here I am today, eighty-five
> years old![13]

By the way, when is it appropriate to start boasting about your age?

I mean, when someone turns forty, they try to keep it quiet. When they turn fifty, they only whisper it to a few friends. But I've noticed that something seems to happen around the age of eighty – they start shouting about it!

Caleb is not keeping his age quiet:

> I am still as strong today as the day Moses sent
> me out; I'm just as vigorous to go out to battle

---

[12] Joshua 14:8b-9.
[13] Joshua 14:10.

now as I was then. Now give me this hill country that the LORD promised me that day. You yourself heard then that the Anakites were there and their cities were large and fortified, but, the LORD helping me, I will drive them out just as he said.[14]

Caleb says: 'I may be eighty-five, but I've got a battle-ready heart.'

I'm still up for the fight. I'm not intimidated by the giants. I'm not fazed by the mountains that surround me. I'm not finished yet. With the Lord's help, I'll take this land!

Random question: Have you ever been out for a meal and found that everyone eats at different speeds? Have you found that if you're doing most of the talking, you end up with more left on your plate, while other people have a clean plate?

And have you ever had one of those awkward moments where the server in the restaurant comes and takes your plate because they think you're finished because everyone else is finished and you have to say, 'I'm not done yet. I'm not finished yet'?

Well, that's the story of Caleb in a nutshell!

Everyone must have thought he was *done*, but he wasn't *done* yet. I'm sure everyone thought it was time for him to enter retirement, but he wasn't finished yet!

---

[14] Joshua 14:11-12.

Caleb says, '[I might be] eighty-five years old [but] I am still as strong today as the day Moses sent me out; I'm just as vigorous to go out to battle now as I was then.'

Last couple of verses for now:

> Then Joshua blessed Caleb son of Jephunneh and gave him Hebron as his inheritance. So Hebron has belonged to Caleb son of Jephunneh the Kenizzite ever since, because he followed the LORD, the God of Israel, wholeheartedly.[15]

Don't you just love that? Joshua, his best mate of forty-five-plus years, *blesses* him, not with a gold watch for his retirement, but with a new battle to fight. He blesses him with a mountainous land that's full of giants!

Not a normal gift to give an eighty-five-year-old, but it was exactly what Caleb wanted. He knew that he wasn't finished yet.

Caleb knew that you can retire from a career, but you can't retire from a calling. He knew that God had called him to fight for the land and to defeat the giants, and even though he had to wait forty-five years before he was given the opportunity to fight, he still maintained a battle-ready heart.

It's interesting that when we face battles in our own lives we still use the metaphors of giants and mountains. When we face challenges, we still talk of Goliaths that need to be defeated and mountains that need to be moved.

It wouldn't take any prophetic insight on my part to realise that there could be many of you reading these

---

[15] Joshua 14:13-14.

pages who are facing your own giants that need to be overcome, or have mountains ahead of you that you are praying will be moved.[16] As you read these words, I want to invite you to approach those giants and mountains with a battle-ready heart. Not with a heart that is intimidated, but with a heart that is convinced of God's power and God's promise to fight on your behalf.

I'm inviting you to live with a battle-ready heart.

And my guess is you are asking, 'How do I get one of those?' 'How do I get a heart that says, "I'm not finished yet, but I'm ready for the fight"?'

'How do I get a battle-ready heart?'

And my guess is (I know I'm doing a lot of guessing!) that some will think we get a battle-ready heart by hyping ourselves up. We listen to a motivational talk. We listen to some music that inspires us. We put the *Rocky 4* soundtrack on repeat until we feel like we're ready to fight (which is, of course, what I would do, because there's nothing better than the *Rocky 4* soundtrack!). Or we listen to a dynamic motivational preacher because we believe that they can shout us into a state of greater faith (which, again, I would probably do!).

But, no matter how amazing *Rocky 4* is and how great preachers are, they are not the key to getting a battle-ready heart. The key is found somewhere else.

Let me suggest this principle to you:

The posture of your heart is determined by the position of your mind.

---

[16] Mark 11:23.

What do I mean by that?

Well, if you take time to read Numbers 13 and 14, you will see that the people's hearts sank because their minds were focused on the giants (apparently, the Anakites were a nation of super-tall warriors!).

You might say that their minds were consumed with the problem rather than the promise.

Caleb was different. He maintained his focus on the Lord. That's all that was at the forefront of his mind. He wasn't thinking about the giants. He wasn't looking at the mountains that surrounded him. His mind was set on the Lord, and His power and promise. Nothing else!

So, let's say it again:

The posture of your heart is determined by the position of your mind.

You know, throughout the Bible, the writers of Scripture tell us that the heart and the mind work in tandem. What you focus your mind on impacts the condition of your heart.

Can I give you an example?

In Colossians 3 the apostle Paul writes:

> Since, then, you have been raised with Christ,
> set your hearts on things above, where Christ
> is, seated at the right hand of God. Set your
> minds on things above, not on earthly things.[17]

---

[17] Colossians 3:1-2.

Notice how Paul tells us that the posture of our heart is inseparably linked to the position of our mind. It's like he's saying that if you want a heart that is full of heaven's reality, first your mind must be directed away from 'earthly things' and directed towards heavenly things.

A second example, maybe?

Consider Paul's famous words on the subject of anxiety and prayer in Philippians 4:

> Do not be anxious about anything, but in every situation, by prayer and petition, with thanksgiving, present your requests to God. And the peace of God, which transcends all understanding, will guard your hearts and your minds in Christ Jesus.[18]

Notice how Paul suggests that peace in our heart also requires peace in our mind. The heart and mind work in tandem.

One final time:

The posture of your heart is determined by the position of your mind.

Your heart will sink if your mind is consumed by the giants, but your heart will be ready for battle if your mind is focused on the Lord.

And while this sounds like an aspirational way to live your life, you may be asking, 'How do I actually do that?'

---

[18] Philippians 4:6-7.

Well, I have found Frank Laubach's suggestion that we play a 'game with minutes'[19] really helpful. He promotes the practice of challenging ourselves to direct our thoughts towards God as many times as we can in any given day. We then, at the end of that day, reflect on how many times we've remembered that God is with us. We literally try to count how many times we've placed God at the front of our minds during the course of our day.

Laubach suggests that we keep score and then try to improve upon that score the next day. He deliberately calls this a game because, even though it is a serious spiritual practice, it is also a delight. What could be better that redirecting our thoughts towards God on multiple occasions throughout an ordinary day?

Of course, this needs to be a grace-filled practice. We shouldn't beat ourselves up if one day we achieve a low 'score', but we should take delight in the days when we start to notice that our mind is forming a new habit of repeatedly returning its focus towards God.

I use that word 'habit' deliberately because our minds are formed by the repeated thought patterns that we adopt. Whether those patterns are intentional or accidental, when our minds habitually return to a specific thought, they are shaped by it. This can be as trivial as repeatedly thinking about chocolate, and as serious as repeatedly thinking about a painful experience.

Can I invite you to adopt a new habit? Intentionally direct your thoughts towards God as many times as you can throughout your day.

---

[19] F Laubach, *Letters by a Modern Mystic* (London: SPCK, 2011), p83.

Make Him your first thought of the day.

Turn your attention to His presence that surrounds you as you travel to work.

Pause and give thanks for your meals.

Talk to Him when you're taking a shower.

Notice Him when you are alone in a crowd.

Breathe a prayer as you visit an elderly friend.

Let gratitude well up inside you when you see a beautiful sunset.

Whisper the name of Jesus when you're doing the washing-up.

Hold an internal conversation with Him while you're taking a walk around the local park.

Make Him your final thought of the day.

I have found that people who have made a conscious decision to fix their thoughts on God throughout the day are more likely to wholeheartedly trust in His power to protect and provide for them.

The Old Testament prophet Jeremiah is rarely promoted for his positive outlook on life. He actually became known as the 'Weeping Prophet' because his circumstances were so bad and his depression was so heavy. Tradition suggests that the book of Lamentations is a collection of his poetic writings. It's not a happy book. It doesn't contain many verses that you put on fridge magnets or screensavers.

There's one passage where Jeremiah tells us his story. He describes how he was beaten, tortured and left for dead. Then he writes:

> Yet this I call to mind
> and therefore I have hope:
> Because of the LORD's great love we are not consumed,
> for his compassions never fail.
> They are new every morning;
> great is your faithfulness.[20]

Did you notice how Jeremiah was intentional with his thought life? Even though his life was incredibly tough, he chose to direct his thoughts towards God. He created a habit of 'calling to mind' that God is faithful. That He is compassionate. That His love is great. That every new day is a gift of His grace.

If you want a battle-ready heart, you must arrange your days around the practice of the presence of God,[21] around moments where you fix your thoughts on Him. Moments where you remove your thoughts from the giants that intimidate you and place them on to the God who surrounds you.

---

[20] Lamentations 3:21-23.

[21] See Brother Lawrence, *The Practice of the Presence of God* (Eastford, CT: Martino Fine Books, 2016).

For many centuries, Christians have adopted another practice called Fixed Hour Prayer.[22] One expression of that practice is to do something David demonstrates in Psalm 55 where he says, 'Evening, morning and noon I cry out in distress, and he hears my voice.'[23] David would pause three times a day, bring God to the forefront of his mind and call out to Him.

If you find the 'game with minutes' a bit too intense, would you give Fixed Hour Prayer a try?

How about aligning your schedule with your values, deliberately pausing three times a day and bringing God to the front of your mind?

Make it the first thing you do in the morning; try to find even five minutes where you sit quietly, or read a psalm, or whisper the name of Jesus under your breath.

And then take some time around the middle of the day. Take a walk around the block. Take some bathroom solitude. Shut your eyes at your desk (if that doesn't make you look too weird!). For five minutes in the middle of the day, set the Lord before you.[24]

And then, at the end of the day, before you close your eyes to sleep, instead of scrolling social media or watching the latest news update, pause for five minutes and bring God's power and provision to the front of your mind and dwell on that so that you sense His presence surround you.

---

[22] I discovered this concept by reading P Scazzero, *Emotionally Healthy Spirituality* (Nashville, TN: Thomas Nelson, 2006), p157.

[23] Psalm 55:17.

[24] See Psalm 16:8, ESV.

Would you give that a try?

And would you let me be a little more direct?

In order for this to work for you, you will probably need to do three things:

One: Put your smartphone in another room, because your smartphone is possibly the biggest enemy of your spiritual growth right now.

Two: Switch off Netflix (at least, press pause!) because it's possible that what you are watching on Netflix takes up more space in your mind than God does.

Three: Slow down. Remove some of the unnecessary activities from your life, reduce the hurry level and take some deep breaths, so that you can direct your thoughts towards God. At least for five minutes.

And for those who are ready to move on to graduate level stuff and find Fixed Hour Prayer simple, how about taking the 86,400 seconds of every day and living as many as you can with an awareness of God and with your mind directed towards Him?

The reality is, your thoughts cannot be empty. If your mind is not centred on God's promises and power, you will be entertaining thoughts about giants that are stronger than you and mountains that are bigger than you, and your heart will sink. Your heart will melt. There is no such thing as an empty mind.

Eighty-five-year-old Caleb embraced the fight ahead of him, but he chose not to allow the giants to take centre stage in his thought life. Caleb chose to place the goodness, the power and the promises of God at the forefront of his mind. And the result? He approached the fight with a battle-ready heart and claimed his inheritance.

My prayer for you?

That when giants and mountains attempt to intimidate you, your heart will be battle ready; you will have trained your mind to be God focused; you will know how to 'set the LORD always before [you]';[25] so that your heart will remain steadfast and strong.

That's battle-ready, wholehearted living right there.

Habits for the heart

Do you ever sit down to pray and your mind wanders?

Do you ever sit down to pray and your mind doesn't wander?

That's probably a better question!

I make it a daily habit to intentionally sit in stillness in God's presence for ten to fifteen minutes. I try to focus my mind on His presence that surrounds me and fills me. I try to allow Him to love me and to allow my heart to reflect this love back to Him.

Then I think about my to-do list.

Then I think about what I'm going to have for dinner.

Then I think about an idea for a sermon.

Then I remember that I'm praying.

You too?

---

[25] Psalm 16:8, ESV.

Well, here's a simple practice that might help. Some traditions refer to it as Centring Prayer:[26]

1   Find a place where you can sit quietly for ten minutes or so.
2   Close your eyes, take a few deep breaths and become aware of God's presence with you.
3   Repeat a simple word or phrase that centres your thoughts on God. It might be something like 'Jesus' or 'Father' or 'I love You, Lord'.
4   Return to that sacred word whenever you notice sounds, thoughts or images have distracted you.
5   Let the silence be your prayer.

If your mind keeps on wandering (and it probably will), don't beat yourself up; rather, see each distraction as another opportunity to redirect your thoughts towards God. If you spend ten minutes in silent prayer and your mind wanders ten times, you have ten opportunities to focus your mind on God's presence and to remember that He is with you.

Ultimately, your heart will be so grateful that you are experimenting with this habit. Your heart is overstimulated and will love the silence and the stillness that this practice brings. So persevere with it. Your heart will thank you one day!

---

[26] This is taken from my own experience, and from reading a variety of books about prayer.

3

A Heart That Sees

Online customer reviews.

A blessing or a curse?

Any time I'm heading towards a restaurant or booking a holiday, that's the first place I go to. Before I part with my cash, I want to know what I'm letting myself in for.

But it's not as simple as that.

As you know, one person can visit a hotel and report that the service is first class; that the hotel is clean, modern and serves the best food in town.

The next person tells a different story. It's dirty, outdated and the food is inedible.

Two people can experience the exact same thing and yet come back with two totally contrasting reports.

I guess it depends on what you are looking for and how you've trained your eyes to see.

Jump back into Numbers 13 and 14.

After escaping Egypt where they had been held as slaves for 400 years, Moses and the people find themselves on the border of the land God has promised to them. Moses arranges for twelve leaders to go and spy out the land, and as they go he gives them some instructions: 'I want you to check out how many people there are in Canaan; how strong they are; the kinds of towns they live in; the quality of their soil; and if there are any grapes, would you bring some back so that I can taste them?'

Moses never asks them to make an assessment as to whether they think they are strong enough to defeat the Canaanites. All he asks for is some facts and figures.

He doesn't ask for an opinion, just the details.

After forty days, when the spies return, they give Moses the details. They speak of grapes and giants.

'It's true! It certainly is a fertile land. The grapes are massive... and so are the people, there're some big guys out there. Big grapes and big people!'

They give Moses the details. The facts and figures.

Then their tone changes. Instead of just giving Moses the news, they give him their perspective; their report.

You know as well as I do that there's a big difference between the news and a report. The *news* is the facts and figures. A *report* provides a perspective on the facts and figures.

The first is information. The second is revelation.

The first is what you think. The second is how you see.

The news tells us that thousands of people are escaping a war-torn country for their safety. One report tells us that these refugees are coming to take our homes and steal our jobs. Another report explains that this is a perfect moment to demonstrate humanitarian care and concern for those in great need.

The news gives the hard data.

The report reveals the heart condition of the reporter and how that heart condition influences the way they see their world.

Moses asks the twelve spies for the news which then develops into a report. As we know by now, two give a good report; ten see things differently.

Picture the scene:

Joshua and Caleb walk into the camp and with big smiles on their faces shout with joy, 'You should see the grapes! They are massive! This is a land of blessing. We can do this! (Oh! By the way, there are some giants there too!)'

The ten spies walk into the camp and with fear on their faces they explain, 'You should see the giants! They are massive! We can't do this! (Oh! By the way, there're some big grapes there too!)'

Fascinating, isn't it?

Two groups of people can experience and see the exact same thing and yet come back with contradictory reports. Both groups had travelled together. They saw the same people, the same land, the same soil and the same towns. But their reports sounded like they hadn't spent even a moment together. How does that happen?

Well, let me offer a suggestion.

It's not about *what* you see, but it's *how* you see it.

The other ten spies used the wrong measure to assess the situation. They measured their chances of success by their own weaknesses rather than by God's strength.

'We are teeny-weeny little grasshoppers and they are massive giants who could just lift one foot and squash us whenever they choose.'

Joshua and Caleb saw things differently. They assessed the situation by looking at it through the lens of God's strength. They could see a God who saved Noah's family from a worldwide flood; a God who saved Jacob and his family from a widespread famine; a God who parted the Red Sea so that they could walk to safety on dry land; and a God who provided water and food and clothes as they walked towards freedom.

They assessed the situation with stories of God's power in the forefront of their minds. It meant that their hearts could see things differently. So they gave a good report and declared, 'We can do it!'

The twelve spies stood before Moses and the people. They presented the news; the facts and figures. Then they offered two differing reports. They said, 'You choose!' 'You choose between the good report and the bad report. It's up to you!'

I appreciate what I'm just about to write is a nice Christian cliché, but I'll write it anyway because I believe it contains some truth:

The report you believe is more important than the news you receive.

The report you believe can shape your future more than the news you receive.

The report you believe can have a greater hold on your life than the news you receive.

Perhaps an illustration might help?

A few years ago now I read a statement written by a gentleman called Wayne Grudem. Professor Grudem has been one of the world's leading evangelical theologians for a number of decades. His writings on systematic theology have been used as a textbook in most Bible colleges, including my own. He has a PhD in NT Studies from Cambridge. He was the general editor of the ESV Study Bible,[27] which contains around two million words. I've listened to many of his podcasts on systematic theology, which he communicates with great humour and insight. If my brain is the size of an orange, his is the size of a planet.

Back in 2015 he was diagnosed with Parkinson's disease and he wrote how he was finding it harder to use a keyboard, to button his shirts and to concentrate on his work. This disease has no known cure and therefore his condition must be managed for an unknown period of time.

That's the news. Those are the facts and figures.

From this news he could have formed a bad report or a good report.

As I read his words, it seemed to me that he had decided to believe a *good report*. Not that he was pretending that his illness wasn't real or that it wasn't really serious, but his words portray a deep faith in his God. He writes with a heart that sees the presence of God in his trials:

> My hope of a perfect, Christ-like, resurrection body is even stronger now.

---

[27] evangelicalbible.com/esv-study-bible/ (accessed 15th March 2021).

> Parkinson's is a 'light momentary affliction'[28] in the light of eternity.
>
> My personal fellowship with God is far more precious than any measure of physical health, and I deeply and truly feel that right now.
>
> I am at peace.[29]

That's what it means to believe a good report.

It doesn't mean that you pretend that the news isn't real, that there aren't really giants in the land. It means you choose a faith-filled, God-centred perspective. You see that God is bigger than any enemy, any situation, any challenge that comes your way.

The report you believe is more important than the news you receive.

The most heart-breaking part of the Numbers 13 and 14 story? The people chose to believe the bad report. And the result? Forty years of desert wandering with the majority of the people never stepping into their God-given destiny.

All because they chose to accept the wrong report.

Now, that all took place around 3,400 years ago.[30]

What about us today? What does this story teach us?

Well, can I offer you some ideas?

First, be very careful which thoughts you entertain

Imagine the thought process the people must have gone through as they heard the spies' differing reports. They

---

[28] See 2 Corinthians 4:17, ESV.

[29] www.desiringgod.org/articles/i-have-parkinsons-and-i-am-at-peace (accessed 6th February 2021). Permission granted.

[30] www.biblehub.com/timeline/ (accessed 16th March 2021).

would have heard the words, 'We can't,' ten times. They would have heard the words, 'We can,' only twice.

'We can't.'
'We can't.'
'We can't.'
'We can.'
'We can't.'
'We can't.'
'We can't.'
'We can't.'
'We can.'
'We can't.'
'We can't.'
'We can't.'

I wonder which words took root in their hearts?

I wonder which perspective they gave too much headspace to?

Ever found yourself adopting that ten-to-two ratio?

God whispers to us to take on a new challenge, or we are presented with an exciting new opportunity, and in our minds we repeat 'I can't' ten times before we give space for two 'I cans'. We allow the bad report to take root and drain life out of us, rather than believe the good report and walk into the unique destiny God has prepared for us.

I love what the apostle Paul says: 'Whatever things are of good report, if there is any virtue and if there is anything praiseworthy—meditate on these things.'[31]

---

[31] Philippians 4:8, NKJV.

Paul is saying, 'The only thoughts we will allow to stay in our minds are those "good reports" that result in Christ being formed in us. Any other negative reports we will take captive and throw out!'

Paul isn't saying that Christ-followers won't ever hear bad reports; he just says that we will choose not to dwell on them.

There's a strange old saying that goes something like, 'You cannot keep birds from flying over your head but you can keep them from building a nest in your hair.'[32] (I appreciate no one in their right mind would ever allow a bird to make a nest on their head, but hopefully you get the point!)

It's an old saying, but it reminds us of the truth that you and I might not always be able to avoid the bad reports, but we can choose not to give them headspace. We can choose to throw them out and give headspace to thoughts that result in life and hope. Most of us find ourselves living in a culture that is interwoven with cynicism and scepticism. Whenever we see light at the end of a dark tunnel we are told that it's a train coming to knock us down. But wholehearted followers of Christ choose to take their thoughts captive. They resist the bad report and believe the good report.

Second, be very careful about the company you keep
Take a forty-year leap (or so) from Numbers 13 to Joshua 2. Moses has died and Joshua is in charge. History repeats

---

[32] Attributed to Martin Luther,
www.goodreads.com/quotes/757798-you-cannot-keep-birds-from-flying-over-your-head-but (accessed 7th March 2021).

itself and the leader of the people of Israel needs someone to spy out the land.

I imagine Joshua saying to himself, 'I'm not going to make the same mistake as Moses. There's no way I'm going to ask twelve people to give me their opinion. I'm going to be very careful about who influences this situation. I'm going to carefully select just two spies who will give a faith-filled, good report.'

> Then Joshua son of Nun secretly sent two spies from Shittim. 'Go, look over the land,' he said, 'especially Jericho.'[33]

And when they returned from their mission:

> Then the two men started back. They went down out of the hills, forded the river and came to Joshua son of Nun and told him everything that had happened to them. They said to Joshua, 'The LORD has surely given the whole land into our hands; all the people are melting in fear because of us.' [34]

I may have this wrong, but it seems to me that Joshua is being very careful about who he allows to have influence over his own life and the lives of the people that he's leading. He's not going to repeat the mistakes of the past. He's not going to allow people to bring a bad report and jeopardise the mission again.

---

[33] Joshua 2:1.
[34] Joshua 2:23-24.

I have found that if I spend time with people who are negative, people who see things with the eyes of fear rather than the eyes of faith, and who always communicate a bad report, I can soon start to follow their thought patterns and adopt their attitude.

I grew up playing loads of cricket. Every Saturday afternoon, at the local park where I used to play, a group of ex-players would sit on the same park bench and offer their evaluations of the quality of the game and the ability of the players – as well as their perspective on just about anything else that was happening in the world at that time! They became known as 'Critics' Corner' because their perspectives were not exactly positive. You only had to go within a ten-metre radius of their bench and you were likely to be infected by their negativity because it was so contagious.

Do you know people like that?

Do you have a 'Critics' Corner' in your life?

You know, as I read the story of Joshua I can see how he becomes increasingly careful about the company that he keeps. He wants to be surrounded by people who will bring a good report. He loves being with his best mate, Caleb, because he sees life just like he does.

Joshua and Caleb didn't need people around them who pretended that life was easy, they just valued being around faith-filled, God-centred people who could see with the eyes of faith and believe a good report.

Third, be very careful which message you communicate
Take a quick look at Numbers 13:32. Notice how it wasn't enough for the ten spies to bring a *bad report* but they went a step further and gossiped it among the people. 'And they

spread among the Israelites a bad report about the land they had explored.'

Not only did the ten spies lack faith in God and believed that God wouldn't come through on His promises, but they also spread their negativity throughout the community.

I wonder what kind of message you communicate?

You know, I think there are some people who are addicted to spreading a bad report; they just can't seem to help it.

They get a new job and you say, 'Great! Isn't it fantastic that God has given you a new job?' And they look grumpy and say, 'Yes, but it's going to be hard work, and long hours, and I'll have to commute fifteen more minutes a day.' They just can't help but give a bad report.

They get a new car and you say, 'Great news about your new car. God's been so good to you!' And they reply, 'Yes, but the fuel consumption isn't as good as my last car, and the car insurance is £10 more a month, and because it's new I'm gonna have to wash it more and take better care of it.'

They just can't help themselves. They are addicted to spreading a bad report.

Know anyone like that? Are you like that?

What if you were addicted to spreading a good report? What if people loved being around you because you stirred faith and hope in them? What if you had such a big view of God that you motivated people to take faith-steps, to dream big dreams and achieve great goals?

What if the message you were to consistently communicate was the message of a good report?

Fourth, be very careful about the stand you take

As I read Numbers 13 and 14, one thing that jumps out at me is the courage that Joshua and Caleb showed as they swam against the tide of popular opinion in their community. It appears that the vast majority of the Israelites were full of doubts. Full of fear. Full of anger. They could only see one outcome in this situation, and it wasn't good.

Joshua and Caleb were different. They could see what the people couldn't see. Through the eyes of faith, they could see victory. They could see a great big God coming to rescue them.

So they took a stand.

Just the two of them.

Joshua and Caleb stood before the crowd of haters and boldly shouted, 'We can!' and, 'We should!'

Everyone else was shouting, 'We can't!' and, 'We shouldn't!'

Joshua and Caleb took a stand and declared a good report.

Have you noticed something?

Have you noticed that no one remembers those who said, 'We can't'?

Have you noticed that people name their children after those who took a stand and said, *'We can'*?

I've met plenty of Joshuas and Calebs. Not so many Shammuas and Paltis.

Why?

Nobody remembers the names of those who said, 'We can't', but the names of those who said, 'We can,' are etched in history for us all to remember. History will always remember and celebrate wholehearted people who look beyond the problems and see the possibilities.

And my prayer for you?

That you, too, will have a heart that sees.

Habits for the heart

In order to develop a heart that sees God-possibilities, I have found it very helpful to mediate on the Psalms that describe some of His great attributes. As we do this, we come to the point of letting go of our limited concept of God. We let go of that box we have put God into, and we open our hearts to allow God to be whatever He wants to be and needs to be in our lives.

How about starting with Psalm 103?

Find a quiet space and a comfortable seat. Put your smartphone in a lockable drawer. Take a few deep breaths. Read these words slowly. Do it again. And then a third time. How do they help you see God differently; more accurately?

> Praise the LORD, my soul;
> all my inmost being, praise his holy name.
> Praise the LORD, my soul,
> and forget not all his benefits –
> who forgives all your sins
> and heals all your diseases,
> who redeems your life from the pit
> and crowns you with love and compassion,
> who satisfies your desires with good things

so that your youth is renewed like the eagle's …

The LORD is compassionate and gracious,
slow to anger, abounding in love.
He will not always accuse,
nor will he harbour his anger for ever;
he does not treat us as our sins deserve
or repay us according to our iniquities.
For as high as the heavens are above the earth,
so great is his love for those who fear him;
as far as the east is from the west,
so far has he removed our transgressions from
us.[35]

And then, once you've exhausted these words, progress to other psalms, such as Psalm 107, Psalm 113 and Psalm 145.

Sit in the silence and allow the psalmist's descriptions of God to settle in your heart, then start to name your giants and mountains in His presence and notice how you start to see them differently.

---

[35] Psalm 103:1-5,8-12.

4

A Son-shaped Heart

Roman Catholic nun Sister Madonna Buder is a remarkable lady. At the age of eighty-two she became the oldest woman to complete an Ironman Triathlon. That's a 2.4-mile swim, a 112-mile cycle and a 26.2-mile run. Widely considered to be one of the most challenging one-day sporting events, Sister Madonna Buder took it in her stride, finishing the race in a little over sixteen and a half hours. In preparation for the race she trained religiously (of course she did!).[36] You might say, she has the 'spirit' of Caleb upon her!

A little older than Sister Buder, Caleb's approach to life was also wholehearted. He too was no quitter. He kept on fighting; he kept on moving forward with energy until he crossed the finish line.

It's important to be clear at this point that being wholehearted is very different from being hard-hearted. There are some people who run life's race, struggle through life's challenges, overcome many of life's

---

[36] www.thetimes.co.uk/article/meet-sister-madonna-the-86-year-old-iron-nun-8bjjdghgh (accessed 6th February 2021).

obstacles, and cross their finish line with a hard heart. It is the hardness of their heart that has enabled them to endure the knocks of life, but they then finish their lives angry, defensive, bitter, fearful.

Not so with Caleb. He concluded his life with a son-shaped heart.

When Caleb stood on the edge of the Promised Land with the eleven other spies, he saw the future from the perspective of a son. As he looked at the Promised Land, he knew that it was his legacy. It was a gift that was going to be given to him by the God who loved him. In fact, in Joshua 14, when Caleb was given his portion of the land, Joshua told him that Hebron was his 'inheritance'.[37]

It appears that Caleb was ahead of his time and knew something about God that the majority of his contemporaries hadn't discovered: that the God of the universe was his Father. That his heavenly Father was good. That as a son of that Father he was loved and secure. That his Father would fulfil His promises to him and that, just like any good earthly father, his heavenly Father would pass on to him an inheritance.

Caleb had a son-shaped heart. He learned to depend on and trust in the goodness, the favour, the grace, the provision and the promises of his Father God.

There is, of course, another heart shape. We'll call it a slave-shaped heart.

As ten of the twelve spies made their assessment of the land, they adopted a different heart posture. Rather than having son-shaped hearts that trusted in the goodness of their heavenly Father, they had developed slave-shaped

---

[37] Joshua 14:13.

hearts. Rather than trusting in the expansive vision of a vast land that their Father had promised to give them as their inheritance, they chose to believe that they would be better off as slaves.

Let's jump back to Numbers 13 and I'll show you what I mean:

> They came back to Moses and Aaron and the whole Israelite community at Kadesh in the Desert of Paran. There they reported to them and to the whole assembly and showed them the fruit of the land. They gave Moses this account: 'We went into the land to which you sent us, and it does flow with milk and honey! Here is its fruit. But the people who live there are powerful, and the cities are fortified and very large. We even saw descendants of Anak there. The Amalekites live in the Negev; the Hittites, Jebusites and Amorites live in the hill country; and the Canaanites live near the sea and along the Jordan.'
>
> Then Caleb silenced the people before Moses and said, 'We should go up and take possession of the land, for we can certainly do it.'[38]

Have you noticed how Caleb was speaking like a son? He believed that his Father God was giving them an abundant land as their inheritance, and since his Father God had a track record of fulfilling His promises and providing for His people, Caleb had no doubt that they should move forward into the land.

---

[38] Numbers 13:26-30.

But not everyone saw it that way:

> But the men who had gone up with him said,
> 'We can't attack those people; they are stronger
> than we are.' And they spread among the
> Israelites a bad report about the land they had
> explored. They said, 'The land we explored
> devours those living in it. All the people we saw
> there are of great size. We saw the Nephilim
> there (the descendants of Anak come from the
> Nephilim). We seemed like grasshoppers in our
> own eyes, and we looked the same to them.'[39]

It only took ten men whose hearts were controlled by fear to create a culture of fear. To create a culture of unbelief. Even though they had previously witnessed God's miraculous deliverance from Egypt, they could not shake off the mindset of a slave, so they expected pain and punishment rather than provision and protection.

You know, I've sometimes heard people say, 'The reason I struggle with faith is because I've never seen a miracle!' That's understandable. But here is a community that has seen the Red Sea part for them to walk across on dry land (it doesn't get much better than that!). And yet yesterday's faith was not enough to carry them through today's challenges. They say, 'We can't do it.' They spread a 'bad report'. They approach their challenges with a slave-shaped heart.

Can I throw in an extra observation for free?

---

[39] Numbers 13:31-33.

Just because one opinion has a majority of supporters doesn't mean it is right.

Of the twelve spies, ten had slave-shaped hearts and said, 'It can't be done.' Eighty-three per cent of the vote said, 'No. We can't take the land because the giants are too big!' Just because 83 per cent say 'no' doesn't mean they are right!

I know that most of the people who read this book will live in a democracy where you can have your say and the majority view wins the vote. But it's worth pointing out that the kingdom of God is a theocracy. It's only God's vote that really counts!

In Caleb's story, the majority view drowns out God's view, and as a result the people remain in the land of 'just enough' rather than stepping into the land of 'more than enough'. They exist in the land of daily manna rather than enjoying the land of overflow – the land of milk and honey. And it's all because the people adopt the majority view rather than discern God's view – the only view that really matters.

One last look at the story. Jump into Numbers 14:

> That night all the members of the community raised their voices and wept aloud. All the Israelites grumbled against Moses and Aaron, and the whole assembly said to them, 'If only we had died in Egypt! Or in this wilderness! Why is the LORD bringing us to this land only to let us fall by the sword? Our wives and children will be taken as plunder. Wouldn't it be better for us to go back to Egypt?' And they said to each

other, 'We should choose a leader and go back to Egypt.'[40]

If you are wondering what a slave-shaped heart looks like, just read those verses again and again. Rather than embrace the uncertainty of their freedom, they long for the certainty of slavery. *Life was so much better when we were slaves.*

Quick question: Have you ever remembered something in the way it *did not* happen?

Sometimes we call that looking back with rose-coloured spectacles. We look back to an event and, because of the distance in time, we remember it to be loads better than it really was.

If you are currently at school or university and you are kind enough to be reading this book, it's possible that there are some people who are older than you who will say to you, 'Enjoy your school days, they are the best days of your life.'

Do you have anyone saying that to you?

Well, it is possible that they have forgotten what really happened!

The reality is, a few decades have passed since they were at school or university and they have forgotten how painful life was back then, and all they remember are the highlights.

They forget that they had no money as students and so ate tins of baked beans as their only meals for ninety-five consecutive days. They forget that their parents forced them to wear summer uniform all winter, even when it

---

[40] Numbers 14:1-4.

was snowing. They forget they waited six years to pluck up the courage to ask their 'one true love' on a date, and then when they found the courage to ask the response was 'no' and they never spoke to them again.

It's often human nature to put on those rose-tinted spectacles and convince ourselves that the 'good old days' were really good, even when they weren't!

Ten of the twelve spies create a culture of fear, and that culture affects how the whole community thinks. They gather the people together and they say, 'Life was so much better back in Egypt! At least when we were slaves they fed us and kept us alive. The certainty of slavery is so much better than the uncertainty of freedom. Slavery was good. Let's go back!'

While it's easy to criticise their approach, we aren't too different from them today.

That's why you are still dating that person who you know is bad for you. You choose to stick with the certainty of what you know rather than risk the uncertainty of being free from them.

That's why you stick with the job you hate. You would rather stick with the boredom of your daily routine because it makes you feel secure rather than embrace the uncertainty of a new adventure.

That's why some of you are so bored with your life. Every time you get to the edge of starting a new and exciting thing you step back into your boring routine because it feels safe.

Sadly, we often choose the routine and security of slavery rather than the uncertainty and risk of freedom. We stand on the edge of the Promised Land. We stand on the edge of a land of overflow and, because we know that the Promised Land is also a Land of Battles, we say to ourselves, 'Slavery is less risky. Let's go back to Egypt!'

I'm writing this chapter because I believe each person has a choice.

You can choose to live with a son-shaped heart or with a slave-shaped heart. You can choose to see yourself as a son of the Father or as a slave of the Master. You can choose to allow your heart to be shaped by one of those two mindsets.

It's the kind of choice that the apostle Paul describes in Galatians 4 where he writes:

> Because you are his sons, God sent the Spirit of his Son into our hearts, the Spirit who calls out, '*Abba*, Father.' So you are no longer a slave, but God's child; and since you are his child, God has made you also an heir.[41]

… or the words of Paul in Romans 8 where he writes:

> For those who are led by the Spirit of God are the children of God. The Spirit you received does not make you slaves, so that you live in fear again; rather, the Spirit you received brought about your adoption to sonship. And by him we cry, '*Abba*, Father.' The Spirit

---

[41] Galatians 4:6-7.

himself testifies with our spirit that we are God's children.[42]

The apostle Paul seems to agree with me (or, more accurately, I seem to agree with Paul!) that you can either see yourself as a son or as a slave, and how you see yourself has a significant impact on the shape of your heart. Whether you will live wholeheartedly, half-heartedly or even hard-heartedly.

Now, I appreciate that as soon as I say that you need to see yourself as a son, there will be around 50 per cent of you who are reading this book who will struggle to get your head round that idea, because you are female. I must acknowledge that might be slightly weird for you and that's why it's important to explain that when the New Testament describes your 'adoption to sonship', it's not a reference to your gender, it's a reference to your position.

In ancient patriarchal societies, the firstborn son had all the privileges of family life. His father would give him the largest portion of the inheritance and treat him with special honour. And so, when the New Testament calls you a 'son', it's describing the position you hold before your heavenly Father. It's reminding you that you are His treasured possession. That you are incredibly loved by Him. That He loves to bless your life with good gifts and that He has an inheritance prepared for you.

Caleb stands on the edge of the Promised Land, and because he has a son-shaped heart he believes that his Father God is about to bless him with a land that's overflowing with good things.

---

[42] Romans 8:14-16.

The ten spies have slave-shaped hearts and are controlled by a fear of the unknown. They expect defeat, punishment, pain and failure.

Which brings us to the most important question of this chapter: What is the shape of your heart? Son-shaped? Or slave-shaped?

And there's a big difference between the two!

Here's how I see it:

Sons see the *inheritance* while slaves see the *intimidation.*

Sons pursue *intimacy* while slaves only see *instructions.*

Sons long for *relationship* while slaves don't want to break the *rules.*

Sons read a book that encourages them to stop and pray three times a day and they are excited by the opportunity for *intimacy,* while slaves see it as another set of *rules* to fail at.

Sons live by the *law of love* while slaves live by the *love of law.*

Sons embrace *discipline* while slaves fear *punishment.*

Sons think *'expansion'* while slaves think *'restriction'.*

Sons *dream big* while slaves *think small.*

Sons say, *'We can,'* while slaves say, *'We can't.'*

Sons *embrace freedom* while slaves *don't know what to do with their freedom.*

Sons accept *grace* while slaves try to earn *favour.*

Sons receive a *gift* while slaves get *wages.*

Sons have *purpose* while slaves *perform.*

Sons honour their Father through *excellence* while slaves are controlled by *perfectionism.*

Sons believe there is *plenty to go around* while slaves expect all good things to *run out.*

Sons expect *abundance* while slaves accept *poverty.*

Sons are *treasured* while slaves are *measured.*

Sons are *permanent* while slaves are *disposable.*

Sons *love* while slaves *fear.*

I ask you again: What is the shape of your heart? Son-shaped or slave-shaped?

Can I remind you of a familiar story that might just help you answer that question with greater clarity?

We call the story the Parable of the Prodigal Son. It's found in Luke 15. Two sons. One father. You probably know it so well you could retell the story better than me.

I find it fascinating that the rebellious son who wastes his father's money on a crazy lifestyle actually has a son-shaped heart. He knows that his father has an inheritance prepared for him. He knows that his father has land to give him. He knows that his father has an outrageous level of love for him that will chase him down, fight for him and rescue him. Despite his rebellion, the wild son knows how good his father is to him. I would argue that he has a son-shaped heart.

And here's the irony. The older brother, who is obedient and hardworking, sees everything through the eyes of a slave. When his father celebrates the return of his brother, all he can do is compare his performance with that of his brother and say, 'All these years I've been slaving for you and never disobeyed your orders.'[43]

I remind you of that story because having a son-shaped heart has nothing to do with how perfect a life you've been living. And having a slave-shaped heart has nothing to do with you living a rebellious life. In fact, the opposite is more likely to be true. It's more likely that in trying to obey all the rules you'll miss out on the intimacy your heavenly Father wants to have with you. Obedience is good, but it's not the same as intimacy. Obedience alone will never produce in you a son-shaped heart.

So, if obedience alone doesn't produce a son-shaped heart, how do you get one?

Can I offer one suggestion?

I believe that your heart was designed to be shaped by a voice; specifically, the voice of God. If you look back to Genesis 1, it is the voice of God that brings life out of the chaos, out of the nothingness. It is the voice of God that created the world, created the animals, even created you. He spoke and it happened.

Throughout the pages of the Old Testament, God speaks and circumstances change. God speaks and lives are given new direction. And then in the New Testament, Jesus Himself is affirmed by the loving voice of His Father at the occasion of his baptism: 'You are my Son, whom I love; with you I am well pleased.'[44]

Want to know how to develop a son-shaped heart? Allow the voice of your heavenly Father to be the primary

---

[43] Luke 15:29.
[44] Mark 1:11.

voice in your life. I actually believe it's as simple as that. When you block out the voices that speak lies about your identity and your value, and you deliberately tune in to the voice that speaks affirming words of love from heaven, you will be empowered to embrace your freedom and step into your destiny with confidence and with a son-shaped heart.

I think it starts right there.

Habits for the heart

Prayer is listening as well as talking.

That's probably one of the most important discoveries you can make as you invite God to form your heart. It is very difficult to be shaped by the voice of your heavenly Father unless you intentionally pause and listen to what He has to say.

How about trying to pray *without* words?

How about befriending the silence and making the words of Samuel the only ones you use?

'Speak, for your servant is listening.'[45]

Try this...

Find a place where you can be still.

Set a timer (five minutes would be a good start).

Close your eyes and open your hands.

Whisper, *'God, I am here for You. Please speak to me.'*

---

[45] 1 Samuel 3:10.

Wait.

Wait some more.

Write down the words and impressions that come to mind.

Repeat the next day.

Make it a habit that shapes your heart.

5

A Heart That Follows

Followership.

Put that word into the search bar on your Amazon app and you'll get 310 results.

Leadership.

Do the same. Search Amazon. What do you get? Not an exact number because there're too many matches. Once they get to 100,000, they give up counting.

What does that tell you? Maybe we are more impressed with great leaders than we are by great followers. Maybe our ambitions lead us towards leadership and when that goal isn't actualised, we then settle for followership.

We find ourselves in a culture where being a leader has so much more value than being a follower. We place leaders on a pedestal and give little thought to the art of being a great follower.

I'm not the biggest fan of social media, but if I were to choose one form of social media that I like best it would be Twitter. I think that's because it's a little more concise than the endless Facebook posts of people's 200 holiday photos; the messages that people want to communicate to the person they love but could actually tell them face to face rather than involving the whole world in their love life; and the infinite opinions of America's president (rant over!). I love Twitter because it's just a bit briefer.

The thing I find interesting about the differences between Facebook and Twitter is that with Facebook you have *friends* whereas with Twitter you collect *followers*. It appears that the number of followers you amass is directly linked to your importance in life. More followers equals more importance.

At present, after being on Twitter for around ten years I have amassed 676 followers (impressive, I know!). I follow a global megastar; we are very similar in so many ways. Well, at least in one way. He has a Twitter account, just like me. He has 113 million followers. That's a few more than I have.

It seems to me that we exist in a culture where having followers has greater value than being a follower. In contrast, wholehearted living swims against the tide, resists the pull of the culture and places high value on being a follower.

There's a phrase that the Scriptures use to clearly describe one of Caleb's priorities. It allows us to pull back the curtain and reveal a key to Caleb's ability to live a wholehearted life for the long term. He was a follower.

Whether it is Numbers 14 when Caleb was in his forties, or whether it is Joshua 14 and Caleb is in his eighties, Caleb is described as a follower.

Caleb says of himself, 'I ... *followed* the LORD my God wholeheartedly.'[46]

---

[46] Joshua 14:8, italics mine.

Moses says of Caleb, 'you have *followed* the LORD my God wholeheartedly.'[47]

God says, 'my servant Caleb has a different spirit and *follows* me wholeheartedly.'[48]

Here's my theory: if you say something about yourself that matches what your boss says about you and matches what God says about you, it must be true.

Caleb was a great follower. While the majority of the Israelites did their own thing or submitted to popular opinion, Caleb followed the Lord his God.

As we continue to dissect what wholehearted living looks like, we can clearly see the need for us to adopt the heart posture of a follower. And if, like me, you are passionately pursuing that kind of life, there are at least three observations that we should take on board:

First, God was in front of Caleb

I appreciate that this is ridiculously obvious, but you can't follow someone unless they are in front of you.

Caleb couldn't follow God unless God went before him, unless God was in front of him – which, by the way, was a reality that the Israelites became very familiar with.

When they left Egyptian captivity, we're told in Exodus 13, 'By day the LORD went ahead of them in a pillar of cloud to guide them on their way and by night in a pillar of fire to give them light, so that they could travel by day or night.'[49]

---

[47] Joshua 14:9, italics mine.

[48] Numbers 14:24, italics mine.

[49] Exodus 13:21.

And then, later on, as they approach the Promised Land, Moses encouraged the people by saying:

> The LORD himself goes before you and will be with you; he will never leave you nor forsake you. Do not be afraid; do not be discouraged.[50]

To follow the Lord is to do what David does in Psalm 16 where he says, 'I have set the LORD always before me.'[51] It means that He leads. He sets the pace. He gives the orders. He determines the direction.

Again, let me suggest something that's incredibly obvious: if God is not out in front, you are leading, not following. If God is not in front of you, you are hoping that God is tagging along with you wherever you are going. If you are giving the instructions, determining the speed and setting the course, you are leading, not following.

If at any time you are attempting to lead God and are not allowing Him to lead you, your life will feel out of sync. You will soon feel like you are lost. You will feel hurried and harassed because you are not moving at the correct pace for this season of your life.

If that's where you are at, then the wisest things to do is swap.

Let God lead.

You follow.

(And let's be honest, He's a better leader than you anyway.)

---

[50] Deuteronomy 31:8.

[51] Psalm 16:8, ESV.

For Caleb, to follow God meant that God had to be in front of Caleb.

Second, God was moving
I appreciate that this a chapter in stating the obvious, but you can only follow someone if that person is actually moving. You can observe someone who remains stationary, but you can't actually follow them because they're not going anywhere. You observe statues and monuments because they stay where they are. You only follow something or someone that moves.

When we read that Caleb committed his life to following God, he expected God to move. He expected change and adventure and risk and new experiences and new opportunities and new land and new locations. He didn't expect things to stay the same!

Sometimes, when we look back on Church history, we can be tricked into thinking that God's objective in the world has been to create institutions and denominations, because the Church has become akin to a global organisation. We can easily forget that His intention was to birth a dynamic, risk-taking, Spirit-led movement of people that would resist the status quo, push back boundaries, bring heaven to earth and pray for God's kingdom to come.[52] We can easily forget that Jesus commissioned His disciples to move throughout 'Jerusalem … Judea … Samaria, and to the ends of the earth'.[53]

---

[52] Matthew 6:10.
[53] Acts 1:8.

God has always been a God who moves. Our job has always been to keep in step with His movements.

Third, Caleb was moving

If Caleb was a follower and God was in front of Caleb and God was moving, we must assume that Caleb was moving too! We must assume that Caleb expected movement because He was following a God who loves initiating forward momentum.

When Caleb stood on the edge of the Promised Land with the eleven other spies, it never crossed his mind that they should retreat, surrender or stand still, because he was following a God who moves. That's why, when he was eighty-five years of age, Caleb didn't put on his slippers and enjoy a relaxed retirement, but instead said, 'Give me that hill country where the giants live!'[54] because he was still following a God who refuses to stay still.

Followership requires you to step back and allow God to lead you so that when He moves, you move. You listen for His promptings rather than your own good ideas. You choose to orientate the whole of your life around His prodding and provoking. You prioritise listening to His voice over all the other voices that are clamouring for your attention. When He says, 'Go,' you go. When He moves fast, you get your running shoes on. When He slows down, you hit the brakes.

When He moves, you move.

I've heard it said that the two most scary events in a parent's life happen seventeen years apart. The first happens when you put your newborn baby in a car seat

---

[54] See Joshua 14:12.

for the first time, hoping that they are safe and secure as you drive away from the hospital and head for home. The second scary event happens when you give them the keys and you allow them to drive you for the first time!

I've done this twice so far.

It's not an experience I can recommend.

To sit in a car with your teenager at the wheel and have no control over where you're going, at what speed you will travel and whether or not the brake pedal will be applied at the correct time... I've had better life experiences.

I appreciate that this is a very simplistic preacher illustration, but to wholeheartedly follow God is like handing over the keys of your life to Him and allowing Him to drive. He determines the direction and the speed. He determines whether you will stop for the long term or just keep on driving. He determines whether you turn left or right because you're not leading any more, you are following.

A brief note to leaders. The quicker we discover that leading is less about us leading and more about us surrendering and following, the better. Most leaders feel pressure to create a strategy, communicate a vision and move forward with clarity. But mature, wholehearted leaders prioritise surrender over strategy. They prioritise time on their knees, listening for the divine whisper. Before they are leaders, they are followers.

And you might notice that this kind of followership paid off for Caleb. He followed the Lord wholeheartedly wherever He would lead. Caleb fought the giants. He received his inheritance. Life was good for him.

But it's worth noting that it came at a cost.

I guess the cost started when the people who refused to follow God like he did decided to oppose him, discredit him and even stone him.[55]

And then he spent forty years wandering around a wilderness with those same people, waiting for them to die, until there was only Joshua and himself left. For four decades Caleb would walk around the desert burying his friends and family. Burying those who had refused to pursue God with the same level of devotion as he had.

The cost of wholeheartedly following God was high for Caleb.

The reality is, it always has been.

This concept of following God is not reserved for great Old Testament stories. In the New Testament, when Jesus called His disciples, He often used two words: 'Follow Me'.

Jesus called Levi the tax collector as he sat at his tax booth: 'Follow me'.[56]

Jesus called Simon and Andrew while they were catching fish: 'Follow me'.[57]

Jesus called James and John while they mended their nets: they 'followed him'.[58]

To make sure there's no confusion, Jesus made it clear, 'Whoever serves me must follow me'.[59]

---

[55] Numbers 14:10.

[56] Luke 5:27.

[57] Matthew 4:18-19.

[58] Matthew 4:21-22.

[59] John 12:26.

In Jesus' day, there were many followers, many disciples of different religious leaders. The disciple of a Jewish rabbi would have to give up most of his material benefits in order to study the Torah, but he knew that this would only be for a limited time. Later on, once he had graduated and become a teacher himself, he would then reap the financial and material benefits and would lead a comfortable life.

Not so with Jesus.

When Jesus called His disciples to follow Him, they were often called to a life of humility, to simplicity and even sometimes to suffering. Following Jesus meant they had to be willing to leave their homes, their families, their occupations and their securities. They would follow Him to a radical life where they would experience pain as well as pleasure.

Some of the toughest words that Jesus spoke were directed not to His enemies but to those who were to take the challenge of following Him. These were words that spoke about sacrifice, ignoring earthly treasures, carrying crosses and enduring persecution.[60] Of course, we often choose to ignore those words, and opt to only read the bits that make us feel warm and comfortable, but they are right there, front and centre in Jesus' teaching.

In our home, we don't have many verses from the Bible on pictures around our house in the way that some Christians might, but we do have a calendar that has an encouraging word for every day. It always has a verse that encourages us, but there's no sight of the more challenging words of Scripture. There's plenty of, 'I can do all things

---

[60] Matthew 16:24-25.

through Christ who strengthens me,'[61] and, 'nothing in all creation will ever be able to separate us from the love of God'.[62] But they seem to have mislaid, 'In this world you will have trouble,'[63] and, 'Follow me, and let the dead bury their own dead,'[64] and, 'Whoever does not take up their cross and follow me is not worthy of me.' [65]

Strange how that happens!

A number of years ago now, CNN ran a news story about a company that had started to produce religious dolls. They produced dolls of Jesus, Moses, Mary and David. The dolls stood one foot high, cost $24.99 and had hand-sewn clothing, movable limbs and hands that could grip objects. At the push of a button each was able to play back five Bible verses, apart from Moses who recited the Ten Commandments (of course). The dolls were produced so that people would hear the comforting words of the Bible and children could take them to bed and sleep well.[66]

I understand why we do that kind of thing because Jesus' words *do* bring comfort and peace, but we mustn't ignore the reality that the Bible teaches us that there's a cost to wholeheartedly following Him.

For Caleb, there was a cost to following God wholeheartedly. He spent four decades wandering around a place he never wanted to be. He spent forty years

---

[61] Philippians 4:13, NKJV.

[62] Romans 8:39, NLT.

[63] John 16:33.

[64] Matthew 8:22.

[65] Matthew 10:38.

[66] money.cnn.com/2005/04/12/news/midcaps/jesus_dolls/index. htm?cnn=yes (accessed 7th February 2021).

digging the graves of his family and friends; he spent forty years knowing that he should have been in the land of more than enough rather than the land of just enough.

In New Testament terminology, we describe this as 'the cost of discipleship'. And while that may sound a little depressing, I need you to know that there's also another cost. The cost of not following Jesus wholeheartedly. The cost of rejecting His invitation to a life of enterprise and intimacy. I would argue that this cost is a greater one.

I'm thinking of the story of the rich young man whom Jesus invited to follow Him.[67] He offered him an opportunity to begin an adventurous life of followership but his cash got in the way. He walked away from Jesus downhearted because he wasn't prepared to pay the price of discipleship.

But I wonder if he paid a different price.

As an older man, as he looked back on his life, I wonder whether he carried the regrets of a missed opportunity. Did he see the early Church starting to flourish and grow, and think to himself, 'I could have been part of that'? Did he look back and say, 'If only I had taken that opportunity!'?

Imagine the cost to Caleb if he had chosen *not* to follow the Lord God wholeheartedly.

Imagine the adventure he would never have taken. Imagine the battles he would never have won. Imagine the land he would never have conquered. Imagine how he would never have known what it was to walk with God, to be used by God, to be led by God, to know God personally. He would not have known God's miraculous

_____

[67] Matthew 19:16-30.

provision, God's supernatural peace, God's indescribable power.

Imagine the cost to Caleb if he had chosen to do his own thing, chosen his own path and had fallen in love with leading more than following.

You see, there's a cost to followership, but there's a greater cost when you choose not to follow Him wholeheartedly. That cost is the kind of life you miss out on if you choose not to pursue God and run hard after Him.

And so, my prayer for you?

That you will live a wholehearted life, where you ask God to go ahead of you. A life where you passionately pursue Him wherever He leads you. The kind of life where when He moves, you move.

That kind of life will probably cost you big time.

But it will be nothing like the cost you will pay if you choose an alternative way to live.

Habits for the heart

If you're looking for a way for your heart to be formed by followership, there are two words you need to become familiar with: 'surrender' and 'submission'. When we practise these two words, we are freed from the burden of always having to get our own way and be in control. While we should never condone or encourage the act of submission in abusive relationships, in healthy relationships both submission and surrender provide us with the freedom to give way to others, hold their interests above our own, allow them to lead and, in return, we become first-class followers.

Try one of these practices as part of your weekly rhythm and see how it starts to shape your heart:

- If you have children, devote the whole of one morning or afternoon to submitting to their will. Ask them how they want to spend that period of time and do it (within reason, of course!). Give them your full attention for the whole of the time. Go where they want to. Play whatever games they want to. Learn how to submit.
- Call a friend. Tell them you would like to spend a day with them doing whatever they want to do. Watch their favourite film. They may choose the restaurant. They can take the lead on every decision and you will follow. Learn how to surrender your will.
- If you are married, offer to do some of your spouse's household chores this week. If they clean the bathroom, you clean it. If they do the ironing, you do it. If they cook, you cook. Find multiple ways to serve them for a day or a week. Discover how being a servant does something good to your heart.

Be creative. Dream up some imaginative ways you can step away from self-centred living and learn to surrender. It will create in you a new kind of heart and you'll become even more comfortable with *followership*.

6

An Unhurried Heart

Toothache.

Ever been there?

A couple of years ago I experienced the worst toothache of my life. It kept me up at night. I was popping large amounts of painkillers in the day. Nothing and no one could solve it. And while there was a massive downside to having toothache, there was an upside. I am now on first-name terms with my dentist.

On my first emergency appointment, I just turned up at the dentist's surgery feeling desperate. I walked into the consulting room and they suggested to me that God must have been looking down on me because someone had just cancelled their appointment and the receptionist had managed to squeeze me in at the last minute. To which I said something like, 'Yes, He is! And I actually believe that God might just sort that kind of thing out for me!'

Because of that slightly odd and religious response, my dentist actually started asking me some deep theological questions while my mouth was full of some strange-shaped instruments that were being used to remedy my tooth pain. Have you ever tried answering a question about predestination while having a dentist's drill in your mouth? I have. By my third appointment in a week, we were conversing like we were best friends.

For a few months I got to know my dentist very well. I also got to know the surgery's waiting room with equal levels of familiarity.

During those months of pain, I sat in that room for a few hours each week trying to concentrate on random articles in the kinds of magazines I wonder if anyone actually reads apart from when they're in dentist waiting rooms, while also trying to avoid direct eye contact with my fellow sufferers who sat quietly around me. While I was there, I started to find it interesting to see the different ways people waited. Some looked anxious, while others seemed relaxed. Some got frustrated, even angry, because the dentist was running late. Others whispered stories to their partners of all the terrible things that their dentists had done to them over the years. Some looked fearful and fidgety. Others appeared chilled and carefree.

I started to wonder what it takes to wait well.

We're now into Chapter 6 of this book and you will have noticed that we've been digging into two key texts from the Old Testament: Numbers 13 and 14, and then Joshua 14. One thing we might have missed is that there's roughly forty-five years between those two passages. Forty-five years between Caleb seeing the land and Caleb receiving the land.

For me, one of the most impressive things about Caleb's story is that he maintains full devotion to God while he patiently waits for his dreams to become a reality. He patiently waits forty-five years for God to fulfil His promise to him, and during that season of waiting he upholds his spiritual passion and remains wholehearted in his faithful dependence on God.

And if you're wondering what forty-five years looks like, look at me.

Earlier in this book I explained that I am a middle-aged man. At the time of writing this chapter I am forty-seven years of age (I would be very happy to be mistaken for a sprightly forty-five-year-old) and so, roughly speaking, Caleb's season of waiting was the length of my life. Add together my pre-school years, my years at infant, junior and senior schools, my years working for a bank, my years studying for a degree, my twenty-plus years on the staff of a local church, and you've got forty-five years.

That's how long Caleb waited.

And he waited well.

In fact, this is his testimony:

> Now then, just as the LORD promised, he has kept me alive for forty-five years since the time he said this to Moses, while Israel moved about in the wilderness. So here I am today, eighty-five years old! I am still as strong today as the day Moses sent me out; I'm just as vigorous to go out to battle now as I was then. Now give me this hill country that the LORD promised me that day.[68]

Caleb had been hanging around for more than four decades, but his belief that God would fulfil what He had

---

[68] Joshua 14:10-12.

promised never diminished. Caleb managed to keep his spiritual zeal red-hot even when there seemed to be little or no sign of forward momentum. There are no signs of impatience or frustration. Caleb waited well.

I wonder, how well do you wait?

Many authors and speakers have gone before me in identifying a common disease that afflicts almost all of us. They call it 'hurry sickness'.[69] It is a pattern of behaviour that is characterised by an inability to be still. We rush. We become addicted to activity. We allow our smartphone to mess with our minds. We are hooked on hurry. Most of us have found that this sense of hurry can be both addictive and exhausting in equal measure. And while I don't suggest that you call your boss tomorrow morning and say, 'I'm taking a day off because I'm suffering with hurry sickness,' I do suggest that each of us acknowledges that there is a sense of hurry in our world that is doing violence to our souls. I think it's worth recognising that there's something that has happened in our culture that has created in us a hatred for waiting.

Of course, there are some trivial symptoms of 'hurry sickness' that aren't too important but still indicate that we have a problem with waiting. That thing we do where we move from one checkout queue to the next as we quickly calculate the potential wait time based on the number of items of shopping the person in front of us has, divided by their estimated age, multiplied by their perceived level of vitality. Or that thing we do when we multitask to the point of forgetting one of the tasks. Or that thing people

[69] www.psychologytoday.com/gb/blog/the-time-cure/201302/hurry-sickness (accessed 8th March 2021).

do when they go to sleep in their daytime clothes in order to save time in the morning (do people actually do that?).

There are some forms of waiting that are pretty trivial, such as in supermarkets and at traffic lights. There are others that are far more serious. There are difficult forms of waiting. The waiting of a childless couple who desperately want to start a family. The waiting of a person who wants to have work that is meaningful and significant and yet cannot seem to find it. The waiting of a deeply depressed person who longs for a morning when they will wake up wanting to live. The waiting of the person who took a leap of faith and is now hoping that God will step in and do what He promised.

I wonder what you are waiting for.

You see, every one of us, at some juncture of our lives, will have to learn to wait, and it may just be one of the hardest things we are called to do. It is also possible that what God does in us while we wait is as important as what it is that we are waiting for. It's possible that waiting is not just something we have to do while we get what we want, but it's part of the process of becoming what God wants us to be, because while we wait, God works.

In Numbers 13, with wholehearted faith, Caleb sees what is possible. With wholehearted faith, he trusts in God's promises. But it's not until Joshua 14 and after forty-five years of waiting that Caleb receives what has been promised to him.

My question to you is, 'How does someone do that?' How do you remain wholehearted in your devotion to God in a season of waiting, when things aren't moving ahead as fast as you had hoped?

Well, let me attempt something slightly foolish. In a chapter that's all about slowing down and taking our time, can I give you seven very quick observations that I believe will help you cultivate a heart that waits well?

1. Keep the story alive

I love how, in Joshua 14, when Caleb is in conversation with his mate Joshua, he has the story of what happened forty-five years previously on the tip of his tongue:

> I was forty years old when Moses the servant of the LORD sent me from Kadesh Barnea to explore the land. And I brought him back a report according to my convictions.[70]

During seasons of waiting, one of the things that can happen is that the story of what God has said or God has done can fade. Sometimes there can be a sense of shame because of our lack of progress, and so, instead of keeping on talking about the story, or sharing the story, we allow the story to fade and die.

About ten years ago I talked with the leadership team, and then the congregation at the church I serve in Coventry, and said I had sensed the Holy Spirit whisper to me that we should make plans to touch the lives of 1,000 people on a Sunday. I explained to them where I was when I heard God speak to me, what I sensed Him say and the impact it had on me. As a result of that prompting, and after much prayer from our leaders, we took steps to hold multiple Sunday services and then moved to a local

---

[70] Joshua 14:7.

theatre to hold our gatherings. While we have experienced some numerical growth towards that goal, at the time of writing we have not gathered with 1,000 people, in person, on a Sunday. And because that promise has taken longer than I hoped to be fulfilled, I have stopped telling that story and sharing that vision. I think I was probably embarrassed by the length of time it was taking for that dream to become a reality and so I just stopped speaking about it.

In a time of waiting it's essential that you keep the story on your lips, that you keep the vision alive by retelling the story. Some of you have stories of what God has done in your lives and the promises He has spoken to you. Some of you have a sense that you are on a journey to somewhere significant, but it's taking you longer to get to your destination than you had hoped, yet it's vital that you keep your story alive by keeping it on your lips. Share it again with a trusted friend. Talk about it with your spouse, your parents, your children, your pastor. Outline it again in your journal. Keep the story alive.

2. Remind God of what He said

Again, in Joshua 14, Caleb was reminding Joshua of what had been said to him. He was reminding his close friend and leader of what had been promised to him by Moses:

> So on that day Moses swore to me, 'The land on which your feet have walked will be your inheritance and that of your children for ever,

because you have followed the LORD my God wholeheartedly.'[71]

Obviously, unlike Caleb, Moses hasn't promised anything to you, but it's possible that God has spoken to you. That He's spoken a promise to you. That He's placed a dream in your heart. And, from examples set for us in the Bible, it appears totally appropriate to remind God of what He has said to you. It's not that God is forgetful, it's just that He seems to appreciate His people reminding Him of what He has promised. It's almost like a way we demonstrate to Him that we are trusting what He has said to us – that we are standing on His promises.

In the Scriptures, there are many examples of God's people going to God and reminding Him of what He had said to them, or what He had promised to them. The best example of this principle is found in Exodus 34, where God reveals His character to Moses on Mount Sinai:

> The LORD, the LORD, the compassionate and
> gracious God, slow to anger, abounding in love
> and faithfulness, maintaining love to thousands,
> and forgiving wickedness, rebellion and sin.[72]

This statement then becomes the most quoted verse in the Bible by the Bible, because God's people keep reminding God of what He said. They keep saying and singing and praying: 'God, You said You are compassionate and

---

[71] Joshua 14:9.

[72] Exodus 34:6-7.

gracious and slow to anger; now we remind You to be and do what You promised You would be and do!'[73]

During your seasons of waiting, make it a habit to remind God of what He has already promised to you, because as you do that you are saying to Him, 'I am building my life on what You have said to me.'

3. Maintain your convictions

Remember back to Chapter 2? I suggested that when Caleb explored the land and brought back a good report it was based on his conviction that God is good, that God would fulfil His promises and that God has good gifts to give His children. And so Caleb says, 'I brought him back a report according to my convictions.'[74]

Convictions are our deeply held beliefs or opinions that are almost unchangeable. It's like they run through the core of who we are.

It's possible that at some stage in your life you will have eaten a stick of rock. It's that incredibly sweet, solid stuff that you usually buy from UK seaside towns, and if you eat too much of it, you end up on first-name terms with your dentist, just like me. If you are familiar with this dentist's nightmare you will know that a stick of rock usually has a word that runs right through it, so that wherever you break the rock, you will still see the word – either the name of the town, or a message of love, or a football team.

Well, that's what a conviction is like. It's like, if you were to break a person in half (which I appreciate you

---

[73] Exodus 34:6; Psalm 103:8; Psalm 145:8.
[74] Joshua 14:7.

can't do – but go with the illustration anyway), that belief would run right through everything they do or say. You might have a conviction that 'God is always good and He works in all things for my good', or that 'where God guides He always provides', or you might hold a conviction that 'you can't out-give God'.

In times of waiting it's possible for our convictions to start to erode because when things don't move at the pace we had hoped, our convictions look less true. Can I encourage you, in your season of waiting, to identify your convictions? Name them. Then hold on to them, because if you uphold them, they will hold you up.

4. Ask: Why is God keeping me alive?

This may sound slightly strange, but I think it would be a good thing, during a season when you're wondering why things are moving slowly and life seems to be going nowhere, to find a blank page in your journal and write at the top this question: *Why is God keeping me alive?*

You see, it seems through the forty-five years of waiting, Caleb had a conviction that God was keeping him alive for a reason and so, in Joshua 14, he says, 'Now then, just as the LORD promised, he has kept me alive for forty-five years since the time he said this to Moses.'[75]

Let's assume that God can 'take you out' any time He wants. He gives life and He can take life away. It therefore makes sense that if He's given you life and He's keeping you alive, He's doing it for a reason. In seasons of waiting, those reasons can start to become somewhat obscured, and so, if you are in one of those seasons right now, I

_____

[75] Joshua 14:10.

would suggest that it would be a healthy thing to find that blank page and write at the top, *Ten reasons why God is keeping me alive*, and then to start to create a list!

5. Don't stop moving

Here's another thing I find fascinating: while Caleb spent forty-five years waiting for the promise to be fulfilled, he still joined the rest of Israel as they 'moved about in the wilderness'.[76] He didn't just sit still waiting for something to happen. He kept on moving, believing that as he moved, God would lead him out of the wilderness and into the land that had been promised to him.

Here's something I learned a few years ago: most *promises* from God are *prophecies* that speak about your *potential* and they require your *participation* for them to become a reality. In other words, just because God has promised you something, it doesn't give you the right to sit there waiting for it to happen. You need to take some steps. You need to move.

Here's something else I've learned in recent years – that most promises and prophecies are like automatic doors. You have to walk towards them for them to open up for you!

An example, perhaps?

In January 2019 I sensed an internal whisper from God that the church I help lead should make some significant improvements to its building. It didn't make much sense, because we were hiring a local theatre for our Sunday gatherings that had a large and well-equipped auditorium, but I plucked up the courage to talk to our

---

[76] Joshua 14:10.

leadership team about it. I told them that I sensed the Lord say, 'You should create a facility that will facilitate all that I have planned for your future.' I shared what I thought I had heard from God, we prayed and moved on with the agenda.

Five days later, in the same room where we had previously met together as leaders, we were all together again, this time having lunch with a guest speaker who was ministering to us for the weekend. She has a strong prophetic gift. While eating our sandwiches, this person dropped into conversation, almost as an aside, that she heard God saying to us that we should create a facility that would facilitate all that He had planned for us. Five days apart the exact same words were spoken, in the exact same room, to the exact same group of leaders.

It didn't take a gift of discernment or a PhD to realise that God was speaking to us.

From that moment our leadership team decided to be proactive and walk towards what had been spoken to us. We planned for a full refurbishment of the church building. We started to raise funds. And exactly one year after the prophetic word was given, we started to create a facility that would facilitate all that God had planned for our local church – even though we had no idea what He had planned! The refurbishment was due to be completed by 22nd March 2020.

Does that date sound familiar to you?

It was the first Sunday that churches in the UK were not permitted to gather owing to the Covid-19 pandemic. It became the first Sunday of many where our congregation couldn't meet together in our new-look facility. But what had God done? He had ensured that we had all the technical requirements in place to produce a high-quality livestream from a new broadcast centre that would reach many more people than we were previously reaching in person. We had a wonderful facility that would facilitate all that was required in that crazy season where many churches like ours were figuring out the new normal of online church.

If we had heard God speak and stayed still, we may well have missed out on the miracle.

It is possible that you too have heard from God. It's possible that someone heard from God on your behalf. They spoke a prophetic word and you received it as a reflection of the Father's desire for your destiny. Maybe you've been given promises that God has something great planned for you. You've got faith that God is going to do something significant in your life. And then you arrive at a season of waiting, and the temptation is to drift into inactivity. It's tempting to become like a Noah who hears from God that a flood is coming, and sits back waiting for God to build the ark.

Some of you are believing God for a new job, or better health, or a change in a family situation, or for a loved one to come to faith, and you are expecting God to do all the work. You are sitting back waiting for God to turn up, while God is expecting you to take action and keep moving. He's expecting you to participate by studying to get a better CV, or to eat more healthily, or to forgive someone in your family, or to talk to your loved one about Jesus.

You're sitting in the waiting room, waiting for something to happen, but God is wanting you to do what you can do – for you to add your participation to His promise, because they go hand in hand!

6. Build your strength

Don't you just love what Caleb says as an eighty-five-year-old man: 'I am still as strong today as the day Moses sent me out; I'm just as vigorous to go out to battle now as I was then.'[77]

I'm fairly certain that Caleb wasn't as physically strong at eighty-five as he was at forty, but I'm sure that emotionally, mentally and spiritually he was as strong and as vigorous as he was when he was an energetic forty-year-old. Somehow, even during forty-five years of waiting, he had built some serious spiritual muscle and developed a strong and healthy heart.

Caleb's story reminds me of David who, after being anointed as king of Israel, had to wait more than ten years before he actually sat on the throne. During those years of waiting he faced significant persecution, rejection and disappointment, and yet we're told that David 'strengthened himself in the LORD his God'.[78]

The key to coming out of the waiting room with strength and vigour is the ability to minister to yourself. It is that determination to engage with spiritual practices that will give you some spiritual muscle. I have found that disciplines such as deliberate thanksgiving, listening to worship music, speaking out Scripture and meditating on

---

[77] Joshua 14:11.
[78] 1 Samuel 30:6, ESV.

it are vital for building inner spiritual strength in times of waiting, especially if I prioritise them at the start and the end of my day.

7. Focus on the promise

Finally, can you see what Caleb did all through the forty-five years of waiting? He kept what had been promised to him at the forefront of his mind so that after those long years of waiting he was able to boldly say, 'Now give me this hill country that the LORD promised me that day.'[79]

You will probably find that when you're sitting in life's waiting room your mind will start to fill with all kinds of doubts: 'Did God really say that?', 'Has God forgotten me?', 'Am I believing for the wrong thing?', 'Have I done something wrong?' It's in those moments that it's so important that you take your thoughts captive[80] and you place *the promise* at the forefront of your mind. You meditate on it. You choose to believe it as the truth and reject everything else as lies. You teach yourself that this time of frustration is a time of preparation as you wait for whatever God has for you next. You choose to believe that the waiting is only for a season and that what God has promised will be fulfilled.

When your mind is filled with all kinds of doubts, you focus on the promise.

Caleb lived wholeheartedly for forty-five long years. Those years weren't all years of adventure and excitement. Most of them were years of waiting, but I would suggest

---

[79] Joshua 14:12.
[80] 2 Corinthians 10:5.

that he emerged from the waiting room stronger than when he went in because he did those seven things.

And then, when he had done those seven things, he stepped out of the waiting room and into the hill country ready to fight the giants and claim what he had been promised.

My prayer is that you would do the same.

Habits for the heart

As life gets busier and there are more distractions, I have found it helpful to practise meditating on words of Scripture. I appreciate that some Christians get nervous when we talk about meditation, but we are not engaging in a form of meditation that empties the mind – sometimes called 'detachment' – but rather a form of meditation that fills it – sometimes called 'attachment'.

The authors of the Bible rarely instruct us to read the Scriptures, but many times they teach us to meditate on them. This form of meditation is not practised as a tool to help us relax – although that may be a by-product – it is rather a way to help us slow down, connect with God, listen to His voice and then obey what He says. When we meditate on the words written in the Bible, we come to them, not to study them, but to listen to the living Word that is being addressed to us.

Dietrich Bonhoeffer's description of meditation is far better than mine (no surprise there!):

> Just as you do not analyze the words of someone you love, but accept them as they are said to you,

accept the Word of Scripture and ponder it in your hearts. That is all. That is meditation. [81]

Here's a suggestion to help you that's based on the Ignatian[82] tradition of contemplatory prayer:

- Find a quiet place where you won't be distracted for five to ten minutes.
- Choose a familiar story from the Gospel accounts of Jesus' life.
- Read the story slowly a couple of times and then close your eyes.
- See the story in your mind's eye – visualise the faces and the places.
- Hear the story – listen to the voices and the most prominent sounds.
- Feel the emotions – empathise with the key characters in the story.
- Write about what you experience in your journal.

And for those of you who think you can't meditate? I would argue that you can! I learned a long time ago that if I know how to worry, I know how to meditate. Worry can damage my heart. Meditating on the words of Scripture can heal my heart, so I would rather choose to do that.

---

[81] D Bonhoeffer, *The Way to Freedom* (New York: Harper & Row, 1966), p59.

[82] For more information, see www.ignatianspirituality.com/what-is-ignatian-spirituality/ (accessed 7th March 2021).

7

An Uncommon Heart

Where's Wally?

I'm guessing you are familiar with those larger-than-life books that are packed full of crazy doubled-paged illustrations; hidden somewhere in the picture is Wally, and it's your job to find him. As you know, he's wearing a red and white striped shirt, a bobble hat and black, thick-rimmed glasses. And because he's wearing such eye-catching attire, it should be easy to spot him. But it isn't. He tends to blend in.

You know, we're not too different from Wally! Not that we walk around with red and white striped shirts and bobble hats (at least, not many of us), but we do tend to blend in. One of our greatest temptations is to fit in rather than stand out and be different from the prevailing culture that surrounds us.

One thing I find fascinating about our culture is that the people who are desperate to stand out and *be different* often end up just hanging around with other people who are desperate to stand out and *be different* and they end up just blending in to a group of people who are desperate to stand out and *be different* until they don't look any different at all – if that makes any sense!

When I was at senior school there was a group of kids who didn't want to blend in. They didn't want to wear the latest fashions, or listen to the latest music, or wear the latest brands. They wanted to stand out and be different and so, in an act of rebellion against conformity, they all grew their hair long. They all died their hair black. They all wore black clothes. And the irony was, they just formed another group where they could fit in.

You see, being 'different' isn't as easy as you think. In fact, I would suggest that it has less to do with what you wear, or how you style your hair, or what music you listen to, and much more to do with what's going on in your inner world. It has much more to do with the condition of your heart because the people who really stand out as being different in this world have something so attractive about their inner life that it spills over into their outer life, and everyone around them recognises it and says something like, they have a 'different spirit'.

Caleb sets the standard on this one. The posture of his heart was so good that it became evident to everyone that there was a 'different spirit' about it. Most importantly, it was something that God noticed too. The last six chapters of this book have helped us examine the quality of this man's inner world. We've seen that Caleb's heart was full of patience, faith, courage, resilience, determination and perseverance. The eyes of his heart were fixed on the promises rather than the problems. The posture of his heart meant that there was no room to host a bad report and only space to promote a good report. And because

Caleb possessed all those inner qualities, God identified him as a man with a 'different spirit'. And because he had a 'different spirit' God then promoted him and gave him the inheritance he longed for.

This concept of a 'different spirit' stems from just one verse that you can find in Numbers 14:24. At this stage in the story, Moses is trying to negotiate with God about who should go into the Promised Land. God is so angry at the people's unbelief that He threatens to wipe them out entirely, but Moses says something like, 'God, that wouldn't look good! Our enemies would laugh at us and at You!' So God relents, and He says, 'No one who has treated me with contempt will ever see [the land]':

> But because my servant Caleb has a *different spirit* and follows me wholeheartedly, I will bring him into the land he went to, and his descendants will inherit it.[83]

If you are the kind of person who underlines your Bible, you might want to pull it out right now, locate Numbers 14 and then underline those two words, 'different spirit'. If you like to set personal goals for your spiritual life, why not make those two words your target?

The goal? Live with a 'different spirit'.

Just for clarity, that word 'spirit' is not a reference to the Holy Spirit; it is a reference to Caleb's inner life, to the depths of his inner being. Some scholars suggest the words 'spirit' and 'heart' can be used interchangeably, that they are roughly speaking about the same thing: the inner

---

[83] Numbers 14:23-24, italics mine.

part of your life that then overflows to impact the outer part of your life.[84] Caleb had a 'different spirit'; or to use alternative terminology, you might say he had an 'uncommon heart'.

It seems that, in many ways, Caleb sets the benchmark for the rest of the Hebrew Scriptures. From this point onwards, it appears that God is always on the lookout for people who live wholeheartedly; women and men who have a 'different spirit' so that He can promote them and lead them into a place of blessing and a position of influence.

One such person who comes to mind is Daniel. As a teenager he is forcibly removed from his homeland and taken into exile in Babylon. The king of Babylon, Nebuchadnezzar, destroys Jerusalem, taking the sacred contents of the temple and placing them in the temple to his own pagan gods. He then takes the brightest and best of the Jewish elite to serve him in his palace. Daniel is one of those elite individuals. He spends the rest of his life living in a foreign land with a foreign culture. He serves three different kings with diligence and builds an excellent reputation for himself.

By the time Daniel arrives at eighty years of age – at a similar stage of life to Caleb – his colleagues, who are also his avowed enemies, attempt to build a case against him and remove his privileges and position. The reality is, they struggle to find anything of corruption or incompetence in his conduct. In fact, as they try to find words to discredit

---

[84] www.bibletools.org/index.cfm/fuseaction/Topical.show/RTD /cgg/ID/12826/Heart-Spirit-Interchangeable.htm (accessed 7th March 2021).

him, they end up expressing that 'an excellent spirit was in him'.[85]

Daniel's enemies, those who wanted to downgrade his status simply because he was a Jew who had been given a high position, attempted to find inconsistencies that would discredit him, but in the end, they could only say that he had an 'excellent spirit', which is slightly ironic since he was originally selected because he was super-intelligent and incredibly handsome. He was a man 'without any physical defect'[86] and yet, sixty-plus years later, people weren't talking about his looks or his brains; they were talking about something much deeper than that. They spoke about the quality of his inner world.

Daniel had an 'excellent spirit'.

Caleb had a 'different spirit'.

Something about the atmosphere in the interior life of those two Israelite legends made them stand out from the crowd. And it seems to me that when God identifies people with a similar healthy inner world, He then entrusts them with greater responsibility and maybe even greater blessing in their outer world.

Would you take another look at this chapter's key verse?

> *Because* my servant Caleb has a different spirit
> and follows me wholeheartedly, *I will* bring him

---

[85] Daniel 6:3, NKJV.
[86] Daniel 1:4.

into the land he went to, and his descendants will inherit it.[87]

Notice how the sentence is constructed.

God says, 'Because ... I will ...'

Because you have that kind of heart posture ... I will do this for you; because you stand out as having a different spirit ... I will bless you with the land.

This may sound slightly controversial, but this verse makes me wonder whether there are some blessings and some responsibilities that can only be entrusted to people with a certain heart posture. Not everyone has developed the right kind of heart that can carry certain levels of blessing. Some people's hearts are so unhealthy that when they receive a blessing it destroys them rather than promotes them.

You see this principle at work many times with lottery winners. They have been blessed with a large amount of money, but the condition of their heart doesn't match the level of the blessing they have received, and so they waste their wealth, fall out with their family and go into debt. Their heart posture hasn't caught up with the level of their blessing.

Now, please don't misunderstand me. I'm not suggesting that if you live a wholehearted life, God will automatically make you financially rich. That's not how it works. I do, however, believe that God is on the lookout for people to bless. Sometimes we call this His *favour*. Favour describes the way God demonstrates His delight in us. It labels the tangible ways He reveals that a person

---

[87] Numbers 14:24, italics mine.

has His approval. And while this may include financial provision, our God is a multifaceted God and there are a multitude of ways He chooses to bless His wholehearted people.

I believe that God wants to place the weightiness of His blessing on to every person's life, but if there are fractures in the foundations of their inner world, that person's life won't be able to carry what's placed upon it. If I have a divided heart, if I am half-hearted, it may be that my heart isn't ready for the blessing to be placed on it.

It's possible that some of us are saying to God, 'Why am I not living in the land of milk and honey? Why have I not received the blessing you promised to me yet?' And it's feasible that one of His responses may be, 'Your heart is not ready for it yet.'

God said about Caleb, 'Because His heart is ready... because he "has a different spirit and follows me wholeheartedly, I will bring him into the land" and give him his inheritance.' Caleb's heart was ready to receive what had been promised to him.

My hope for you, as you've been reading this book, is that you will experience a stirring in your spirit to live like Caleb. I know that as I studied the story of Caleb and sat in a variety of coffee shops to write this book, a desire stirred in me to develop my heart so that God would say of me, 'My servant Duncan has a different spirit and follows me wholeheartedly.' I've been stirred in my spirit to be like Caleb who was both ready for the battle and ready for the blessing.

And my hope is that you've been having similar thoughts to me; you've been saying to God, 'I want to follow You wholeheartedly.' My guess is that most of us – including the author – know we've got some distance to go before we reach that goal. In fact, we may be wondering if it's even possible for our hearts to change from what they are now so that, one day, we can say we are living with wholehearted devotion to God.

Over the last decade or so, as I've incorporated a rhythm of physical and spiritual disciplines into my daily routine, I've found that these two dimensions of my life often overlap. I've found that I can turn running into praying; that while my body is engaged in activity, my heart is opened up to commune with God and hear His loving voice. And so, I've discovered that if I have healthy physical routines, they aid my spiritual health, and vice versa. In addition, I've found that the principles I employ to keep my physical heart heathy and strong can also be applied to creating a strong and healthy spiritual heart.

In particular, I've found it helpful to take the principles of marathon training and apply them to my understanding of how the human heart can change so that it becomes fully devoted to God.

See it!

First, if you want to live wholeheartedly, you need to *see it*. You need a vision of what wholeheartedness looks like. I've run the London Marathon four times. Each time I've trained for that marathon I have run around the streets of Coventry, and in my mind I would literally visualise running past Buckingham Palace and down The Mall, crossing the finish line feeling strong and full of energy (the second part of that vision never actually happened, by the way). All great sports psychologists teach their pupils to envision what success looks like; to *see it*.

You need to be able to *see* what it would look like for you to live with wholehearted devotion to God. You need to see how that would affect your work life, your family life, your devotional life and your leisure time. You need to see how it would affect your decision-making, how you spend your money, where you travel and what you study. You need to see how it would affect your behaviour, your character and your attitude. If you are going to live wholeheartedly, the first step is to envision what that would look like so that you know what you're aiming at.

Be deliberate

Second, if you plan to live with a heart that is fully devoted to God, you need to *be deliberate*. I sometimes refer to this part of the process as 'advance decision-making'. In order to run a marathon without descending into a dishevelled sweaty mess and passing out at mile twenty, the runner needs to have had hundreds of training runs, some of which are done in terrible weather conditions. I've found the only way I will get out of bed and head out into the blizzard is when I make a decision ahead of time that I will do it. I actually go to bed at night with my running gear and trainers at the side of my bed so that when the alarm goes off, I can fall out of bed, get dressed and get running. I know that I need to be intentional. I need to be deliberate, otherwise my training will drift.

It's the same with your heart. A key question of spiritual formation is not actually, 'Can my heart change?' but, 'Who or what will I allow to change my heart?' and 'Will I allow my heart to be shaped deliberately or accidentally?' The reality is, our hearts are always being shaped or moulded by something or someone, and therefore I know I need to make a decision in advance about how I allow that formation to happen.

I believe that most of us allow our hearts to be formed unintentionally. We adopt passive habits where we operate on autopilot, allowing external influences to shape our hearts without us even noticing it's actually happening. I would even dare to say that the technology you have in your pocket is currently playing a big part in that.

From a variety of online surveys, I understand that if you have a smartphone it is highly likely that you will touch that phone more than 2,500 times a day and that nearly 90 per cent of us check our phones as the first action of our day (technically it's the second action, because the first action is the opening of our eyes!).[88] I don't need to tell you that the content on that piece of technology is shaping your heart and your mind. Whether you're addicted to answering emails, checking eBay, updating your social media feeds, ticking off your to-do lists or watching YouTube, many of us have hearts that are being shaped in a way that has never happened before in the history of the world.

---

[88] www.networkworld.com/article/3092446/we-touch-our-phones-2617-times-a-day-says-study.html (accessed 16th March 2021).

Let's do a quick exercise together: take out your smartphone, locate *settings*, scroll down to *battery* and click on it. You should then be able to see where you're spending most of your time and the kinds of things that are currently unintentionally shaping your heart.

I appreciate there are loads of positive things to celebrate about the advancement of technology in our lifetime, but I would argue that our inner worlds are being unintentionally shaped by the mobile devices that have quickly become our closest companions. Our hearts are becoming hurried and distracted, and we need to start living with some intention and become more deliberate about what or who we allow to form our hearts.

Get some tools

Third, and finally, we need to *get some tools* to help us change. Every time I train for a marathon, I buy a new pair of trainers and some new running kit and I print out a sixteen-week training schedule that I try to stick to religiously. That schedule incorporates shorter and faster runs as well as slower and longer runs. It includes sprints and hill runs, stretches and ice baths. These are the tools that will help me build endurance, stamina and strength.

What happens in the physical is mirrored in the spiritual. There are activities, disciplines and spiritual practices that shape our hearts. As we adopt these tools they help develop a heart that's full of devotion to God.

We can list those tools fairly easily. We can practise *simplicity* so that the hold that materialism has on our hearts is broken. We can practise *solitude* so that the noise of the world is silenced, enabling us to hear God's voice. We can practise *prayer* so that we cultivate a God-dependency. We can use the tool of *fasting* so that we are not controlled by our bodies' desires. The list could go on.

As this chapter heads to a conclusion, here's a question for you to think about carefully: What are the intentional spiritual tools that you are engaging with that are shaping your heart so that you experience the loving presence of God and so that a different spirit is formed within you?

Can I make one suggestion?

I appreciate what I'm about to suggest to you is old school and has been rejected as being too legalistic or too restrictive, but I believe the best habit you can adopt if you want to live with a conscious awareness of the presence of God and develop an uncommon heart is called a 'daily quiet time'.

I know some of you want to be more spontaneous than having a daily quiet time. There's a lot to be said for being spontaneous, but there are some things you can't be spontaneous about. You can't be spontaneous about paying your rent; if you only pay your rent when you feel like it, it's called eviction. You can't be spontaneous about turning up to work on time; if you only turn up when you feel like it, it's called unemployment. You can't be spontaneous about your marriage; if you only talk to your spouse when you feel like it, it's called divorce. You get the point.

There is nothing more important in your life than your relationship with God and the formation of your heart. It's highly unlikely that this will happen accidently or spontaneously, and one of the best tools I can recommend is a daily quiet time.

You may ask, 'What is one of those?'

Well, the clue is in the title. It's *daily*, which means it's something you do every day, as best as you can. It's *quiet*, which means that your smartphone will need to be surgically removed from your hand, and you sit in stillness before God with a Bible and a journal. It's a space and place without distractions. In fact, you don't have to say many words, just say to God, 'I'm here for you,' and trust that God is waiting there for you with open arms. Finally, it's a portion of *time*; and if you're new to this thing, start with five or ten minutes. You don't need to spend hours doing this, just start really small and build from there.

I can almost guarantee you that, if you allow this to become a daily rhythm for the remainder of your life, you will never be the same again. Your heart will be shaped in Christ-likeness and you will become known as a person with a *different spirit*.

Habits for the heart

When I wrote the previous chapter, I did something that I would like to encourage you to do. I found a blank page in my journal and I wrote at the top of the page, 'What does it look like for Duncan Clark to live with wholehearted devotion to God?' Would you do the same? (Just remove my name and add yours, because if you don't, that would be weird!) In fact, I actually believe it would be helpful to repeat this practice every year. Why not start each year by examining your heart and answering this question?

Here's what I wrote:

What does it look like for Duncan Clark to live with wholehearted devotion to God?

- a life of instant obedience to the Father's voice
- a life where I finish as strong as I start
- a life where intimacy is more important than influence
- a life where I'm more at home in the secret place than on the platform
- a life of intention, not a life of drifting
- a life where no area of my life is off limits to God
- a life where I maintain my *first love* for the long term
- a life where living by faith is the norm
- a life of pursuit
- a life of surrender

By the way, I would love to hear what you wrote! Let me know how you're seeking to live with an uncommon heart.

8

Guard Your Heart

'Money doesn't grow on trees, you know!'

I can vaguely remember having that conversation with each of my children, but I'm not 100 per cent sure when it was. My wife, Helen, and I have four children. We're now at that point in life when our children are starting to leave home. University to begin with and then, I would imagine, they will spread their wings a little further and will eventually fly the nest completely. I will miss them greatly when they go, but I appreciate that the process we are going through is part of a healthy family life. Children need to grow up and learn to stand on their own two feet.

It wasn't that long ago that our two oldest children headed off to university for the first time, and it caused me to experience a period of self-reflection. Did I do enough? Had I taught them everything they needed to know in order to flourish in the big wide world? I had distant memories of the 'birds and the bees' chat. I could remember the 'you must support West Ham United if you want to be part of this family' chat. I could even recall the conversation that went something like, 'Money doesn't grow on trees, you know!' But I was left wondering, did I miss out anything important?

Those conversations with my children have caused me to reflect on another conversation that a father had with his children many centuries ago. The father's name was Solomon. In that conversation he wants to distil all the wisdom and knowledge that he has accumulated over the years and then communicate it to his boys so that they will know how to survive and thrive when their father isn't around any more. He tells them to pursue wisdom, to avoid evil, to listen to inspired instruction and to obey godly commands. He wants each of them to live a full and a long life.

As the conversation draws to a conclusion, he pulls them closer. It's like he says, 'If everything I've taught you thus far has gone in one ear and then out of the other, remember this':

> Above all else, guard your heart,
> for everything you do flows from it.[89]

From all the wisdom Solomon had accumulated over the years, from all the ups and downs of life, from all the diverse experiences and encounters, Solomon places this insight and instruction at the top of his list:

> Boys, this is the number one thing I need to leave you with: place a guard around your heart as if it is the most valuable possession that you have.

---

[89] Proverbs 4:23.

It's worth saying something about the word 'guard' that Solomon uses here. It's my understanding that he had in his mind a soldier who would stand at the gate of a city or a town and they would decide what would be allowed into that city. The guard would keep out people with contagious diseases. They would make sure disruptive criminals didn't get through the gate. The guard would keep out anything that might pollute the city. And then the guard would also take responsibility for allowing good resources and healthy people into the city. Anything that would be of benefit for the well-being of the people would be allowed through the city gates.

Solomon gathers his sons around him. He points to the guard on the city gate. He says to them, 'You see that soldier? You need to do for your heart exactly what he's doing for our city. You need to keep out anything that will damage your heart, and you need to allow anything into your heart that makes it healthy. Boys, that is the most important thing I can teach you right now.'

Now, here's where I speculate a little.

I wonder if Solomon had acquired this wisdom, not only from his own experiences, but also from the traditions that he had been taught from childhood. The Israelite people had an expectation that the stories of their ancestors would be passed down the generations so that they could gain wisdom from the failures and the successes of those who had gone before them.

I wonder if Solomon had been told the story of a man who had lived roughly 500 years before him. A man who had fought for their land. A man who trusted God when others had doubted. A man who followed God wholeheartedly for the duration of his long life.

I wonder if Solomon had been told about Caleb.

It's slightly speculative, I know, but I don't think it's totally unrealistic to think that when Solomon gathered his sons around him to pass on his principal instructions concerning life and faith, that he had a hero like Caleb at the forefront of his mind; a hero who had placed a guard around his inner world so that he could live from the overflow of a healthy and a whole heart.

It makes me wonder, if Caleb could live the entirety of his life wholeheartedly, what did he need to guard his heart against? And equally, it makes me wonder what we need to guard our hearts against if we too are going to follow God with a whole heart for the whole of our lives?

Guard against a hard heart

The Bible says a great deal about people who live with hard hearts. There are a good number of instructions from God to His people that they should avoid stone-like hearts that develop because of cynicism, judgementalism, bitterness, scepticism, unforgiveness and the like.[90] The New Testament also picks up this theme, repeatedly warning people to avoid hard hearts that are shaped by religion, selfishness and pride.[91]

I can imagine hard-heartedness was a significant temptation for Caleb. He was the one who had believed

[90] Psalm 95:8 is a good example.

[91] See, for instance, Ephesians 4:18.

God. He was the one who had the ability to get a vision and run with it. He could see what God could do. And he was surrounded by people who didn't have his level of faith. They couldn't see what he could see. When that kind of thing happens, it's very easy to become judgemental of others – to look down on them for their lack of zeal while allowing personal pride to take root.

One of the greatest challenges for people who take their faith seriously is to avoid developing a hard heart. As they seek to live a holy life, to increasingly seek God in prayer, to worship more passionately and to give more generously, they can be filled with a damaging level of pride that results in them becoming judgemental towards others who have not achieved their so-called high standards.

That hardness of heart then overflows into their words and actions. They speak negatively and critically about other people. They are slow to demonstrate forgiveness. They are quick to judge others. They soon become arrogant and selfish.

This kind of hard-heartedness is not just reserved for those who make judgements of other people's perceived faith levels and lack of spiritual vitality. It doesn't take much for us to become hard-hearted towards those who don't work as hard as we do, or don't exercise as much as we do, or don't have the same body shape as we do. While out running, it can be easy to feel superior to those at home, lying on their sofa watching Netflix. A hard heart isn't far away from anyone who puts themselves on a pedestal and then looks with disdain on those who haven't reached their high standards.

Caleb was a man of faith, fight and vision. He was surrounded by a people who were short-sighted and spineless. He would have to spend forty years living with these fickle people, and the only way he could remain wholehearted was by carefully guarding against the hardening of his heart.

Guard against a hurting heart

Not only could Caleb have justified feeling superior to the people he was living with, but he could have also felt justified in harbouring bitterness and unforgiveness towards them. It was their fault that he was aimlessly walking around the desert for forty years. If the people had listened to Joshua and Caleb, they would have stepped into their destiny. Instead, they would spend four decades marching around a lifeless desert; divided and devoid of purpose. And it wouldn't have taken much for Caleb's heart to be polluted with self-justified anger and resentment.

There will be some of you reading this book who have been let down by close friends; you have been betrayed by members of your family; you have been criticised and judged harshly by church members; your marriage partner reneged on the promises that they made to you. You are experiencing pain in your inner world and it's not your fault. You have a hurting heart.

Although I fully sympathise with anyone whose heart is hurting, it can get to the stage where the bitterness, anger and unforgiveness so pollute that person's heart that the hurt wells up inside and spills out in words of revenge and actions of transference. You criticised me, so I'll criticise you. You gossiped about me, so I'll gossip about you. You cheated on me, so I'll cheat on you. And if that person cannot take revenge on the person who hurt them, they will take their pain and transfer it on to someone else who has nothing to do with their hurt. Another person just becomes an outlet for their pain.

This game of revenge ping-pong can easily become the unintentional occupation of anyone who has a hurting heart, and we must guard against it if our heart is to remain healthy and whole. It appears that Caleb would not allow personal hurts to ruin the condition of his heart.

Guard against a harassed heart

I'm talking here about someone who is never at peace. They never know what it means to have contentment in their hearts. I'm describing the person who always wants the next thing or the new thing. Their heart is never at rest.

Caleb was aware that there was a new land ahead of him. He knew that the land contained new levels of blessing for him and his people. But there is no sign in the biblical narrative that his longing for the new thing robbed him of his peace until he received it. While the people around him complained and took God's provision for granted, his heart remained content while he patiently waited for the next thing.

We live in a culture that suggests that we always need something else to make us happy. We must have the next thing or the new thing in order to feel satisfied with our progress. The trouble is, when we spend our lives pursuing the bigger house, the smarter car, the thinner waistline, the higher-paying job and the more exotic holiday destination, our hearts never find a sense of peace. All they feel is harassed, agitated and pressured.

We need to learn the word 'enough'. It's very easy to say. It's not so easy to allow that word to make its home in our hearts.

When I was a child, I received 20p pocket money per week (yes, it was the 1970s), and I thought that if I could accumulate £1, then I would have enough. Until I had £1. And so I got a newspaper round, and I earned £3 a week, and I thought I had enough. Until I had my first real job, working for a bank, and I was paid a whopping £8,000 a year and I thought that would be enough. Until I had my first role working for a church and I was paid £10,000 a year and I thought that would be enough. Until I was ordained by the movement I still serve, and I was given a 25 per cent pay rise, and I thought that would be enough. Until…

I think you get the point.

Hearts become harassed when they don't know how to say 'enough'; when they are addicted to the pursuit of the new and the next. Caleb had his eyes on the prize ahead of him, but there is no sign of it tainting his heart. He was grateful for his daily bread (or manna!) and allowed God to be the source of his contentment. He placed a guard around his heart.

You and I have been on this planet long enough to know that pride and self-centredness are always knocking at the door of our hearts. We've been around long enough to know that we will be criticised, that people will say unkind things about us, and they may even take deliberate action to hurt us. And because many of us are ambitious and driven, we will often be wanting to move on to the next thing and then the next thing and then the new thing. And so, unless we carefully guard our inner world, we could easily develop a hardened, hurting and harassed heart.

This raises an important question: how do we do that? How do we guard our hearts? Well, can I suggest three ways I've sought to guard my heart against those three heart conditions?

Guard against a hard heart by remembering grace

It's all about grace. There are days when I convince myself that I am good enough, or that I deserve all the good things that I have in my life. And then I wake up to that delusion and I remember that everything I have and all that I am is a gift of God's grace. His grace in me. His grace working through me. I come to Him in weakness, not strength, and His grace makes me complete.

Never forget grace.

The moment I feel self-assured and that I've *arrived* is the moment pride starts to pollute my heart. The moment I lose my appreciation for grace is the moment I feel that I've made it and my heart grows hard towards those who haven't worked as hard as I have, or lived the holy life that I have. And my hard heart causes me to feel superior. It causes me to look down on those who haven't achieved my high standards.

I have found that a deep appreciation of grace keeps my heart soft. Tender towards God and tender towards people. It helps me empathise. It moves me to act with kindness towards those who are struggling through life. It reminds me that we are all wrestling with our weaknesses, our frailties and our failings. Grace softens my heart.

There is nothing uglier in life than a person with a hard heart. But one of the most beautiful things you will observe is a person with a soft heart. Don't mistake them for a wimp. Their inner world is so strong that they can cry with those who are mourning, as well as laugh with those who are rejoicing. Their hearts are strong enough to overlook an offence while being soft enough to show Christ-like compassion for the person who is drowning under the consequences of their own sin. They can do this because they have never lost sight of grace.

Guard against a hurting heart by keeping short accounts

I learned a very simple, yet important, lesson more than twenty-five years ago that still affects how I live my life today. My wife, Helen, and I were going out at the time (that's what dating was called in the 1990s!) and at the end of one of our dates we had some kind of argument. To this day I have no recollection of what we disagreed about; all I can remember is that I drove Helen back to her home, dropped her off and then drove away at high speed in my Ford Fiesta 950cc without saying goodbye. I think we call that approach to conflict 'passive aggressive'. I arrived back at my home and my parents could sense that there was something wrong. I explained that Helen and I had had a disagreement, that we hadn't resolved it and I had driven away in a bad mood because I, of course, was right and she was in the wrong. At that point, my dad didn't allow me to take my shoes off or take a seat. He just said,

'Go back.' He told me in no uncertain terms to get back in my car, drive across town, knock on Helen's door, apologise and sort it out. I did as I was told, and we all lived happily ever after.

That day I learned a principle that the apostle Paul didn't need a paragraph to explain; he took just twelve words: 'do not let the sun go down while you are still angry'.[92] I've come to understand this as the principle of short accounts. Rather than allowing hurts, disagreements, arguments and conflicts to fester and do damage to my heart, I've learned to deal with them quickly. I've learned to keep short accounts with people. To apologise speedily. To forgive promptly. To do my best to resolve relational conflict before the day is done.

I appreciate that this approach may sound too simplistic and, without doubt, there are some serious matters that can take a long time to resolve, but I have found that a high percentage of relational conflicts can be quickly eased by a speedy 'sorry', or a quick, 'It's OK, I forgive you.' And I have found that every time I allow the sun to go down while I'm still angry, the deeper the bitterness becomes and the more complex the path to reconciliation turns out to be. Guard your heart by keeping short accounts.

Guard against a harassed heart by giving thanks

I cannot overstate how important living a life of gratitude is if you want to live with a healthy heart. I have found that gratitude breaks a sense of entitlement off my life, especially during those times when I think I deserve more

---

[92] Ephesians 4:26.

than I have already accumulated. I have found that gratitude prevents me falling into the comparison trap when I scroll through social media and I see a friend or a colleague (or a random stranger, for that matter!) with more than I have. I have found that gratitude repels that sense of discontent which tells me that I don't have enough, and creates a feeling of harassment in my heart.

For many years I've practised a spiritual discipline that only takes a couple of minutes a day but has transformed my heart. I don't think this discipline has an official title, so we might call it 'counting your blessings'. It's not complex. It's something that the smallest child can do. It just requires you to stop listing all the things you don't have and list the things you do have. List the things you take for granted. List the physical and material blessings you have received. List the spiritual blessings that are yours in Christ. Give thanks for heat and light. Give thanks for daily bread. Give thanks for grace. Give thanks for chocolate. Every day, create a thanksgiving list.

There is no better way to guard your heart from the internal harassment that discontentment brings than a daily dose of deliberate gratitude.

Solomon was right (of course he was, he was the wisest man around!); the only way you get a heart like Caleb is when you place a guard at its gate. The only way to keep your heart healthy for the long term is to be very intentional about what you allow into your heart and what you keep out of your heart. It's the most important thing of all: 'Above all else, guard your heart, for everything you do flows from it.'

Our God is a heart-God and his primary concern is your heart; so guard it well!

Habits for the heart

An important spiritual practice for those who are serious about guarding their hearts is called an 'inventory'. It's an uncomplicated way of identifying whether you've allowed things into your heart that are polluting it and that therefore need to be confessed, repented of and made clean.

It's very simple…

Find a blank page in your journal and write at the top of the sheet:

What is in my heart today?

With an awareness of the presence of God, pause and ask yourself these questions:

Have I allowed anxiety into my heart as a result of not fully trusting God?

Have I allowed unforgiveness into my heart as a result of carrying an offence?

Have I allowed idolatry into my heart as a result of not putting God first in my life?

Have I allowed discontent to trouble my heart as a result of my ingratitude?

Have I allowed hardness to form in my heart as a result of my lack of appreciation of grace?

Use these questions, and others that may come to mind, to perform an inventory of the condition of your heart. Use the blank page of your journal to keep a record of what you find there.

Finally, conclude this practice by using the words of these psalms as your prayer:

> Search me, God, and know my heart;
> test me and know my anxious thoughts.
> See if there is any offensive way in me,
> and lead me in the way everlasting.[93]
>
> Create in me a pure heart, O God,
> and renew a steadfast spirit within me.[94]

---

[93] Psalm 139:23-24.
[94] Psalm 51:10.

Epilogue

A couple of years ago I had the wonderful privilege of being one of the guest speakers at a conference that was attended by nearly 2,000 young people from all around the UK. It was a great honour to receive this invitation. The conference organisers had created a glossy brochure giving details of all the guest speakers who were invited during the week. Alongside the names and the photos were details of each person's achievements and qualifications. This person has a PhD from the University of Oxford (not me!). This person has a church of thousands (also not me!). That kind of thing.

After the conference I reflected on that brochure and the statements it made. I realised it said a lot about each person's accomplishments and nothing about the condition of their hearts. It didn't say, 'This speaker has a heart full of joy.' It just said something like, 'This speaker has a master's degree in theology.'

Why do we do that kind of thing? I think it's because we have a tendency to be impressed by people's minds and less concerned about people's hearts. If they can think quickly and speak intelligently, we will overlook the condition of their hearts. If they have charisma, we will overlook their character flaws.

God sees things differently. Yes, He wants us to love Him with our minds, but He's more impressed by our hearts. We look on the outward appearance while God takes a deep look into our hearts.[95] In fact, even now, His eyes are looking across every continent of the earth in order to find people who have hearts that 'are fully committed to him'.[96]

God is on the lookout for people who are wholehearted.

It seems to me that when God looks at your CV He looks beyond your qualifications, your strengths and your experiences, and He looks at your heart. It appears to me that when God decides to promote an individual, the number one thing He looks at is the condition of their heart. It's not that intelligence and hard work and talent and gifts and experiences are unimportant, it's just that for God, these things are not His primary concern. We tend to place greatest value on the things that matter least, while placing least value on the things that matter most.

Why did God choose Caleb? Why did God promote Caleb? Why did God bless Caleb with the land?

Simple. He could see into his heart. He could see that this man stood out from his peers and would follow Him wholeheartedly for the whole of his life.

My prayer for you is that, like Caleb of old, you will do the same. You will pursue the Lord your God wholeheartedly each and every day that the Lord generously gives to you as a gift.

---

[95] 1 Samuel 16:7.
[96] 2 Chronicles 16:9.

I pray that, as you live from the inside out, your heart will overflow with courage, faith, resilience and boldness.

I pray that you won't just 'start well', but you will also 'finish well'.

I pray that you will have a battle-ready heart; that the eyes of your heart will be focused on the promises more than on the problems; more on God than on the giants.

I pray that you will see yourself as a son of the Father rather than the slave of a Master and therefore expect Him to give you good gifts.

I pray that you will place God in front of you and determine that you will follow Him wherever He leads at whatever cost is required.

I pray that in times of waiting, you will have a heart that is full of patience and you will live with a quiet trust.

I pray that you will be 'different'; that there will be something about your heart that means you stand out from the crowd.

I pray that you will guard your heart so that it will only be full of things that give you life.

I pray that you will step out of the wilderness and into the land of promises; that your heart will be ready to carry the 'weight' of all the blessings that the Lord wants to place on your life.

I pray that you will accept the invitation to choose wholehearted living for the long term.

And, because I lead a Pentecostal church, it would be my custom to ask that all God's people who have read this book say with me...

Amen!

Appendix

Discussion starters

Heart transformation doesn't just take place in solitude and silence, but also through community and conversation. Why not connect with a few friends, read a chapter or two together and then discuss the ways God is speaking to you about living a wholehearted life? If you meet with the same group of people regularly, you could start every meeting by asking this question:

- How is it with your heart?

And then move on to these discussion questions which will help you along the way towards wholeheartedness as you address each chapter in turn:

Chapter 1: Wholehearted
- When you read that full devotion to God requires the whole of you, does that make you feel uncomfortable? If so, why?
- If it's true that we live from our hearts, why do we then give priority to the development of our minds?

- Wholehearted living 'has nothing to do with striving and everything to do with surrender'. What do you think is meant by that statement?
- What is it about your current stage of life that makes wholehearted living particularly challenging?
- If you are someone who writes a journal, share with your group the kinds of things you've been writing about recently.

Chapter 2: A Battle-ready Heart
- If the health of your heart is determined by the things you allow your mind to focus on, what strategies could you employ to keep your mind focused on things that keep your heart healthy?
- What do you make of the concept of a 'game with minutes'? Have you tried it? Could your group experiment with this practice and report back next time you meet?
- What is your experience of being aware of God's presence throughout the day? Do you ever notice that He's with you, or do you go for weeks without any awareness of His presence?
- If you could explain your regular and repeated thought patterns, how would you describe them?

Chapter 3: A Heart That Sees
- Talk to your group about a time when you experienced an event with another person but you both saw it in very different ways.
- When you read the testimony of Professor Wayne Grudem, what was the first thought that came to your mind?

- What has been your personal experience of the ten-to-two ratio? Do you have a tendency to focus on the negative and struggle to see the positive?
- If your life is heavily influenced by the company that you keep, are there any relationships in your life that you need to rethink? Are there any new boundaries that need to be created?

Chapter 4: A Son-shaped Heart
- Reread this statement: 'we … choose the routine and security of slavery rather than the uncertainty and risk of freedom.' Can you think of areas in your life where that might be true?
- Take another look at the list of differences between sons and slaves. Which of the statements jump out at you and speak into the current condition of your heart?
- As you reflect on the story of the Prodigal Son in Luke 15, what does it reveal about our true sonship in relation to our heavenly Father?
- Christians often speak easily about hearing the voice of God, but it's not always that simple! Share with your group any experiences you have had of hearing God's voice and the ways you're learning to listen to Him.

Chapter 5: A Heart That Follows
- What character traits make a great follower?
- What are the very practical ways you can ensure that God is going on ahead of you and that you are allowing Him to lead?

- Can you share a time in your life when you moved because He moved?
- If you are truly following Jesus Christ, your discipleship will have cost you something. Share with your group the kind of cost you have paid to follow Christ. How does the cost of not following Jesus put this into perspective?

Chapter 6: An Unhurried Heart
- What is in your life that creates hurry in your heart?
- Take a few moments with your group to 'keep the story alive'. Talk to them about the things you are waiting for, and how the wait is making you feel.
- If you were asked to describe your 'convictions', what would they be?
- If David was able to strengthen himself in the Lord during a time of significant waiting, what spiritual practices build spiritual muscle for you while you wait?

Chapter 7: An Uncommon Heart
- In which areas of your life are you most tempted to blend in?
- What does it actually look like for you to live a wholehearted life? Or to live with a divided heart? Or to live half-heartedly?
- As you consider the role that technology plays in your life, how is it sometimes (or often!) a distraction from a deep connection with God? Is there a way you can use it to shape your heart for the good?
- What are the 'tools' that you have found particularly helpful in the formation of your heart?

Chapter 8: Guard Your Heart

- If you had to guard your heart from one thing, what would that one thing be?
- Consider the three heart conditions that are listed in this chapter (hard, hurting, harassed). What are the obvious external symptoms of each condition? How can you notice those heart conditions forming in you?
- How do we balance the joy of seeing God do a new thing in our lives, with the addiction and dissatisfaction that the continual pursuit of new things can create in our hearts?
- Which of the three 'guards' in this chapter most stands out to you and why? Remembering grace? Keeping short accounts? Giving thanks?